# PRA

"It is with unbridled enthusiasm that I demand that you stop what you are doing and read this book! Jo's constant hunger for knowledge as a teacher and her passionate, sarcastic, and unique way of storytelling make her an example to us all to never give up. She gives me hope that we can achieve anything we set our minds and hearts to accomplish, as long as we do it together."

— Vanessa Marcil
Advocate, Philanthropist, & Accomplished Actress

"Joanna Johnson's ideas on teaching come from three places: her heart, her mind, and her experiences in the classroom. I've never known a better educator, and I've been in school my entire life!"

— Ryan Seeley
Principal, Metro Prep Academy

"Joanna skillfully conveys the significance of human connection in both life and learning with her new book! Her exceptional talent for educating others, with a perfect blend of kindness and compassion, distinguishes her as one truly remarkable individual this world needs!"

— Arlene Dickinson
Author, Television Personality, & Entrepreneur

CODE BREAKER INC.

# THAT'S NOT WHAT THIS BOOK IS ABOUT

## JOANNA JOHNSON

# THAT'S NOT WHAT THIS BOOK IS ABOUT

Book design by Brian Aspinall
*www.mraspinall.com*

Cover photo by Elaine Fancy
*www.elainefancy.com*

Breaking code isn't just about programming or artificial intelligence, it's about disrupting the status quo in education. **#CodeBreaker**

| Professional Development | Consulting | Keynotes | Publishing |

www.codebreakeredu.com

To my uncle for making me smart,
My mom for making me brave,
My grandma for making me funny,
And my wife for having the chicken fight.

# ACKNOWLEDGEMENTS

I am deeply thankful for the consistent and unwavering support, encouragement, and guidance that my uncle, mother, grandma, and wife have provided me with throughout the years. Your love and belief in me have been a constant source of strength and inspiration, shaping me into the person I am today.

Special thanks to Jann Arden, Vanessa Marcil, and Arlene Dickinson for your invaluable coaching, feedback, and contributions to this book. Your kindness and advocacy work reach so many. I am forever grateful.

I want to express my deepest appreciation to Ryan Seeley for being an exceptional colleague, mentor, and friend for the past two decades. No matter the journey, I'm proud to ride beside you.

Lastly, I extend my heartfelt gratitude to Brian Aspinall and Code Breaker Inc. for skillfully crafting my story into this captivating and beautifully presented book!

With love,
- JJ

# TABLE OF CONTENTS

# FOREWORD

## BY JANN ARDEN

I somehow managed to stumble across Joanna Johnson one morning as I scrolled through what was formerly known as Twitter. She immediately captured my attention and my curiosity, and I'm very glad she did! Her terse, informative, funny, almost rap-like missives were as entertaining as they were informative. I was hooked on every word she had to say. Having an opinion in today's world comes with a host of baggage and vitriol, neither of which Joanna seemed all that concerned about. She handled negativity with clever and very true jabs back. All of us who have ever dealt with trolls over the past few years were cheering her on from the comfort of our cars and living rooms.

# FOREWORD

Joanna has now taken her unbelievably popular social media Queendom and put pen to paper to cheer all of us on. As an educator, a creator, an artist, a queer champion, a mentor, and a true force of nature, Joanna's new book brings us along on a journey through her life and what indeed made *Unlearn16* who she is today, and perhaps more importantly, why she is.

Her grit and determination to teach young people about the world they live in is inspiring, to say the very least. Her innovative programs and ideas are as vibrant and magical as her personal style. She exudes individuality, which is both refreshing and kick-ass. Being yourself has never looked so good or seemed so appealing, and kids of all ages are taking that big undertaking to heart.

Be who you are, be smart, be brave, be bold, be heard, be fair, be informed. Joanna reminds us on every page that all these things are possible when you have someone in your corner. Joanna's book will end up being a go-to for so many of us. Every second page of mine has ended up with a dog-ear - a morsel of truth, a quick piece of wisdom, a laugh-out-loud paragraph that you will most likely read twice.

Jann Arden is a Canadian singer-songwriter known for her soulful voice and heartfelt lyrics. With a career spanning decades, she has captivated audiences with hits like "Insensitive" and "Good Mother." Beyond her music, Jann is also a best-selling author and a beloved personality, sharing her wit and wisdom with fans around the world.

www.jannarden.com

# PREFACE

# THAT'S NOT WHAT
# THIS BOOK IS ABOUT

**Your decision to read** this book is truly appreciated, and I am sincerely thankful for the chance to accompany you on your learning adventure. While my name may be featured on the cover and in the "About The Author" section, and while the pages are brimming with my stories, it's essential to recognize that this book transcends my personal narrative. Just like a tapestry woven with threads of different colours and textures, each of us carries within us a rich and intricate collection of stories, experiences, and perspectives that shape the very essence of our being. These diverse elements come together to form a beautiful mosaic that reflects our individuality, resilience, and growth. Our stories, whether filled with joy or challenges, our experiences, whether triumphant or difficult, and our perspectives, whether broadened or deepened, all come together harmoniously to weave a unique and vibrant tapestry that shapes our identity and enriches the world around us. This tapestry allows us to explore the depths of our humanity and acknowledge the interconnectedness of our shared human experience. Get ready, because class is in session!

Children perceive the world with a sense of wonder and curiosity. I often wonder if school plays a role in diminishing this in young people. Everything is new and exciting to them, from the colours of a rainbow to the sound of birds chirping. They see the world as a place full of possibilities and adventures, where even the simplest things can hold great significance. Children often view the world through a lens of innocence and imagination, allowing them to see magic and beauty in everyday moments. Their perspective is shaped by their experiences, interactions, and the stories they hear, which all come together to form their unique understanding of the world around them.

In this book you will find stories of my own interactions as a child. Some may prove similar to yours and some may be vastly different. Adult influence on children is profound and far-reaching. As adults, we serve as their role models, shaping their beliefs, values, and behaviours through our words and actions. The way we interact with children, the guidance we provide, and the examples we set all play a crucial role in their development. Our influence can impact their self-esteem, confidence, and overall outlook on life. By fostering a positive and nurturing environment, we can help children grow into compassionate, resilient individuals who are equipped to navigate the complexities of the world. It is important to remember that our influence extends beyond just the present moment; the lessons we impart and the connections we forge with children can have a lasting impact on their future well-being and success.

Creating resilient, kind children involves a combination of nurturing their emotional well-being, teaching them important life skills, and modelling positive behaviour. Encouraging children to express their emotions in a healthy way, validating their feelings, and teaching them coping strategies can help build resilience. Providing opportunities for them to problem-solve, make decisions, and learn from setbacks can also foster resilience. Teaching empathy, kindness, and the importance of helping others can instill a sense of compassion in children. Modelling kindness, patience, and respect in our own interactions with them and others is key in shaping their behaviour. By creating a supportive and loving environment, setting clear expectations, and offering guidance and encouragement, we can help children develop the resilience and kindness needed to navigate life's challenges with grace and empathy.

Within the pages of this book, you will discover tales from my youth that delve into the rollercoaster ride of childhood, the journey of learning, the challenges of teaching, and the complexities of adulthood. My goal is to bring a smile to your face and evoke laughter as you reminisce about your own adventures. Through these shared stories, we may uncover connections through our experiences in education, sports, or even the occasional movie reference, finding common ground that unites us in laughter and nostalgia.

# THAT'S NOT WHAT THIS BOOK IS ABOUT. IT'S REALLY ABOUT THIS:

Our own stories and truths hold immense power in shaping our understanding of the world and our place in it. By sharing our experiences, perspectives, and values with others, we can create connections, foster empathy, and inspire positive change. When we open up about our triumphs, struggles, and lessons learned, we not only validate our own journey but also offer insights and wisdom that can resonate with others. Through storytelling, we can break down barriers, challenge stereotypes, and promote understanding across diverse backgrounds and cultures. When we embrace authenticity and vulnerability in sharing our stories, we invite others to do the same, fostering a culture of openness and acceptance. By being true to ourselves and owning our experiences, we create a space where individuals feel seen, heard, and valued for who they are. This sense of connection and understanding transcends differences and cultivates a deep sense of empathy and compassion among people from all walks of life. Our stories serve as bridges that span divides, offering insights into the human experience and highlighting our shared struggles, triumphs, and aspirations. Through the power of storytelling, we can inspire others to embrace their own truths, learn from diverse perspectives, and come together in solidarity to create a more harmonious and equitable world where kindness, understanding, and respect prevail. In this way, our collective narratives have the potential to not only transform hearts and minds but also drive positive change that benefits society as a whole.

# THAT'S WHAT THIS BOOK IS ABOUT.

# I'M ORANGE & KIDS ARE SMARTER THAN US

**One of my earliest** memories is of three-year-old me gleefully sliding down a metal slide in the middle of winter, wearing a cozy snowsuit that made me look like a little astronaut exploring a new planet. Honestly, I sometimes wonder if that memory is truly mine or if it's a tale my mom has recounted so often that it feels like a cherished part of my own recollections.

Once upon a time, there was a groovy 70s snowsuit that was as bright as a disco ball and as orange as a traffic cone. People couldn't help but stop and stare as I navigated the playground, looking like a funky tangerine snow ninja. Even the snowflakes seemed to pause in awe of this fashion statement, wondering if they should dust themselves in glitter to keep up with the fabulousness. It is a sight to behold, a blast from the past that brings a smile to everyone's face, proving that sometimes, all you need is a little orange flair to brighten up a snowy day.

Funny, isn't it? I often wonder about the distinction between genuine childhood memories stored in the depths of our minds and those that have been woven into our consciousness through repeated family storytelling at holiday dinner. It's fascinating how our perception of history can be shaped by these narratives. But I digress. Let's refocus, Johnson. Back to the story at hand!

Picture this: I stood proudly in my vibrant 1977 orange snowsuit with stylish brown trim, relishing a day at the playground. Meanwhile, my mom, like all parents of the 70s, sat serenely, distanced from the chaos of the sand pit, engaging in lively conversations with the other moms from the community around the periphery of my play palace. She was likely bragging about her new camera which made my orange snowsuit appear pink on film. This was quite possibly the first time a camera had ever been used. As the cold weather kept most playground-goers indoors, only a brave few joined me in our wintry adventure. There was something undeniably exhilarating about that slide, its excitement never fading no matter how many times we slid down. Winter transformed the metal slide into a safer haven compared to its scorching summer counterpart, where the sun at 2 p.m. could turn it into a searing hotbed for bare skin. Who remembers teeter totters, swing sets and merry-go-rounds?

While I was engrossed in play that day, a new arrival, a child around five years old, entered the playground. Here's a little tidbit about me: I

never initiated play with others. Instead, I would linger on the outside, silently hoping to be invited to join in. It's a quirk of mine that I've never quite understood, but perhaps a therapist could shed some light on the matter.

After some time, the five-year-old approached me, introduced herself, and inquired about my name. When I replied, "Joanna," her face lit up as she exclaimed, "I have another friend named Joanna, but she's Black." Perplexed, I glanced down at myself  and my attire and responded, "I'm orange!" We shared a moment of mutual bewilderment before returning to our joyful escapades in the playground independently.

That moment has become a cherished tale in my family, recounted at every Thanksgiving and Christmas gathering for the past 47 years. It's shared not just as a story, but as a symbol of innocence - a child entering a world untouched by prejudice and stereotypes. It makes me reflect: weren't we all once like that? Stepping onto our playgrounds with open hearts, ready to forge friendships, our only distinguishing characteristic is the colour of our snugly zipped snowsuits.

On that innocent day at the playground, no profound lesson presented itself to me, simply because there was none to be had. I had yet to confront the towering peaks of societal indoctrination that lay ahead, waiting to shape my perceptions and beliefs. It was a time of pure simplicity, a fleeting moment untouched by the complexities and biases that would later colour my worldview.

# THAT'S NOT WHAT THIS BOOK IS ABOUT. IT'S REALLY ABOUT THIS:

I'd always wanted to teach senior students. I believed that their intellect and capacity for debate would rival mine. We could engage in long, drawn-out discussions on topics like democratic freedom, civil rights, the motivations for war, and revisionist perspectives on history. And for the record, I've experienced all of that. Older students often seek to have their voices heard because they have valuable insights, experiences, and perspectives to contribute to discussions and decision-making processes. As they mature and gain more knowledge, older students develop a deeper understanding of the world around them and the issues that affect their lives. They want to be active participants in shaping their educational experiences, advocating for changes that reflect their needs and interests. By voicing their opinions and concerns, older students can influence policies, promote inclusivity, and drive positive change within their school communities. They seek to be respected as individuals with unique viewpoints and ideas, recognizing the importance of their voices in creating a more collaborative and student-centred learning environment.

Everyone walks in this world with bias. If someone has the audacity to proclaim they're entirely objective, I can assure you they are trying to manipulate or control. When I first walked into my classroom, I was old enough to command some authority and young enough to think I knew everything - a dangerous combination. With a sense of independence and confidence in my abilities, I felt empowered to assert my opinions and make decisions with conviction. However, this self-assuredness was accompanied by a certain naivety and a tendency to overlook the wisdom and guidance of others. Believing I had all the answers, I sometimes failed to recognize the value of seeking advice or considering alternative perspectives. This blend of authority and overconfidence created a challenging dynamic, where my desire to lead clashed with my limited understanding of the complexities of life, particularly the life of a student in the modern era. Within my first year of teaching high school, I challenged students to debates and shaped my classroom into a space where intellectual discussions and daily debates were integral to our lectures. Yet, deep down, I always assumed I knew more. I had more education, so naturally, I thought I had the best answers (in hindsight, I was too young and inexperienced to know better). Looking back, I was far more inclined to strictly follow educational parameters and textbook guidelines of the day - but let's be honest, we were in the very early era of the internet.

Accessing the latest journal articles still required a trip to the Toronto Reference Library.

Picture this: a group of students embarking on a field trip to the city library for a day of research just after the turn of the century. As they enter the hallowed halls of books and knowledge, their excitement is palpable... until they realize they have to navigate the Dewey Decimal System. Suddenly, chaos ensues as students frantically search for books in the wrong sections, mistaking "Shakespeare" for "Shark Attacks." One student even tries to check out a librarian, thinking they're part of the lending policy. Is that a non-playable character (NPC)? Amidst the confusion, the librarian raises an eyebrow, wondering if she should start a new section on "Adventures in Library Field Trips." It's a day of unexpected twists, turns, and a whole lot of laughter in the quest for research gold. What a time to be alive! P.S. If you don't know what an NPC is, ask your closest teenager.

As I matured, and maybe gained a touch of wisdom, I started to listen more and lecture less. I discovered a penchant for playing devil's advocate, delving deeper into discussions rather than just regurgitating the facts I had learned in my education. It would have been easy to remain fixed in outdated knowledge, resistant to embracing fresh perspectives. However, it was in that realization that I recognized a key aspect of being a good teacher - the commitment to continuous learning and growth.

Do you want to know who taught me the most? The younger students I never wanted to teach in the first place - the Grade 6s, 7s, and 8s. Not the Grade 9s. And if you've ever taught Grade 9, you'll know exactly why I say that. Grade 9 is an exciting time in a student's academic journey. It marks the beginning of high school for many students, where they start to delve deeper into various subjects and explore new interests. In Grade 9, students typically encounter a more challenging curriculum, with a focus on building foundational knowledge and skills for their future studies. It's a time of growth, self-discovery, and new experiences as students navigate the transition to high school and begin to shape their academic path. Grade 9 is a pivotal year that sets the stage for the rest of their high school career.

When I was still a relatively young teacher, I was met with a Grade 7 class that made me contemplate quitting every single day. All educators have those years. The years where we spend every day doing everything we know how to do, and nothing seems to work. Those years when exhaustion falls over you before morning announcements even begin. Individually, they were lovely kids. Collectively, they were like napalm - unfocused, loud, argumentative, impulsive, and quick to lose their tempers. As soon as I had one student settled, another three would riot. Each day would end with them asking, "Did we do better today, Joanna?" or apologizing with "I'm sorry we didn't behave today, Joanna."

You may be wondering why students address me by my first name. This practice isn't a display of disrespect in my school; quite the contrary, it signifies a culture where respect is cultivated through actions and leading by example, rather than formal titles. In this environment, many of our success stories are rooted in the belief that respect is earned through deeds and character. Hence, my students refer to me as Joanna, and in turn, I address them by their first names, fostering a sense of equality and mutual regard in our educational community. This can lead to more open communication, stronger relationships, and a more relaxed learning environment where students feel comfortable expressing themselves.

# I'M ORANGE & KIDS ARE SMARTER THAN US

While I always knew that students didn't come to us each September as blank slates ready to learn and eager to please, I learned a very big lesson that year. Each of my students came to me with their own story of who they were and what they've lived. Until I tried to understand them, their families, their stories, and their pressure points, I would never be able to truly reach them. Until they felt understood and heard, they'd never let me.

One day during fourth period, while I was teaching Grade 10 History, I heard my Grade 7 class preparing to leave their science room two doors down. They were loud, which wasn't out of the ordinary, but I heard a different energy - an urgency I wasn't comfortable with. As I stepped into the hallway, my gaze fell upon a student who appeared visibly embarrassed, seated on the floor, while another student stood in the doorway, chuckling. I saw the student on the floor clenching his pencil tightly, his anger escalating. Just as he began to rise, I swiftly approached and swallowed him with both arms, guiding us through the halls and out of the building. I could sense his heart racing as I settled him down in the parking lot. As we sat together, he turned to me, tears welling up in his eyes, and expressed his gratitude for preventing him from making an incredibly stupid mistake. Later on, I discovered that he had been a target of harassment by the other student and had reached a breaking point. We delved into the root of his anger and discussed the overwhelming feelings he grappled with. While I couldn't claim to have resolved all his challenges, that day marked a turning point for me as a teacher, as I became more attuned to the complexities of my students' lives.

It dawned on me that to be a truly effective teacher, I must hone my listening skills and delve deeper to comprehend my students, often reading between the lines more than I had initially expected. Above all, without a genuine understanding of our students, we cannot hope to effectively educate them. Moreover, it is crucial to acknowledge the immense intelligence of our students; overlooking this fact is the initial misstep of an ineffective teacher.

The following year I was met by young students who would ask questions about everything. How does a battery work? Who discovered how gas is used? Why do countries go to war? Why would people discriminate? Who gets to create school work? Why do we have to take gym class? That last question really poses some ethical and philosophical debates I can't begin to answer in this book. I remember once sitting down with a class of 13 year olds debating and discussing the parameters of free speech. What should be allowed? Where should the lines be drawn? What examples could be used to prove their perspective? How does it impact democracy? What's considered a rational limit? Can you imagine that? So, I took a step that felt right for this modern era - I designed a course specifically for them: Global Issues. This course evolves annually to address current affairs, encouraging critical thinking and debate. It challenges students to conduct research, provide citations, and most importantly, form and defend their own opinions.

At times, we underestimate our youth, seeing them as incapable and lacking intellectual capacity. Yet, they once confidently knew their snowsuit was orange; it is we who have thrown doubt into those simple truths. Hence, I consider it my paramount duty to lead our students back to the certainty of the orange snowsuit - free from bias, internet bots, and any other barriers that may cloud their understanding.

# CLASS IS IN SESSION

## FEATURED VIDEO

# 2

# BERT, ERNIE & MOMENTS OF CHANGE

**In the year 1978,** Superman heralded the era of superheroes, the Lego man came into existence, the Whatchamacallit candy bar hit the shelves, Garfield made his debut in newspapers, and I celebrated my third birthday. I was a loud, opinionated three year old, I know, I know, huge surprise. TikTok didn't make me loud, but it certainly gave me a megaphone. From the moment I was born, my mom made it her mission to instill in me a powerful lesson - that my voice held significance and deserved to be heard. Her unwavering belief in the importance of self-expression and the value of my opinions shaped the very core of my being. Though there were undoubtedly moments when she may have second-guessed her decision to empower me with such a strong sense of voice and agency, I am certain that, deep down, she remains steadfast in her parenting philosophy.

Through her guidance and encouragement, I learned to speak up, to stand tall, and to advocate for myself and others. While my outspoken nature may have presented its challenges along the way, I am grateful for the gift of confidence and self-assurance that my mom bestowed upon me, a gift that continues to shape my identity and influence my interactions with the world around me. I cannot emphasize this enough: Giving a voice to your child, showing them respect, listening to them, and empowering them could be one of the most impactful things you could ever do. That, and ensuring they understand the value of a family vacation spent trapped in a car. One memorable time, my grandma got locked in a rest stop bathroom on our way to Florida, and she genuinely thought we might leave her behind and continue our vacation. But, let's save the vacation stories for another chapter. Now, let's transport ourselves back to 1978 - think shag carpet and you'll be right there.

One day my mom was driving me to daycare, a routine we had followed many times before. This daycare, by the way, was where I learned to perform The "Three Little Pigs" in FRENCH by the age of four! So, every day, mom would drop me off at 6 am - yes, you heard that right, 6 am - so she could head off to work at Wellesley Hospital as a nurse (but that's also a story for another chapter). Our mornings typically unfolded with a serene drive to the daycare. Yet, on this specific day, as we arrived, I made a bold statement by refusing to step out of the car. Let me reiterate: We reached the daycare like usual and I simply refused to exit the vehicle.

My mom didn't raise her voice or show anger; instead, she calmly inquired why I was hesitant to leave the car. I remained steadfast in my decision. This led to a 10-minute conversation, a back-and-forth exchange of questions and answers, until my mom finally unearthed the root of the issue. It turned out that during the short drive from our house to the daycare, I had come to the conclusion that the Bert and Ernie overalls I was wearing that day were only meant for babies. Under no circumstances was I willing to exit the car wearing what I deemed to be baby clothes. The events that unfolded in my mind that fateful morning, the shift in my self-perception and how I wanted to portray myself, remain a mystery. Perhaps I caught something on the radio that my mom missed. But I digress.

At that moment, my mom found herself in a dilemma. I needed to go to school, she needed to get to work, and the ten-minute debate had already limited the options available to her. Could my mom have decided for me? Pulled me out of the car seat and told me the hard facts of life? She could have, but she didn't. Instead, she thought quickly, she thought deeply, she thought of how to respect my feelings yet still get the job done. So in one fell swoop she came up with a solution - a perfect solution.

Mom gazed directly at me and said, "Jo, it's clear these overalls are too young for you. I apologize for not realizing it sooner. But I have a grown-up solution. Would you like to hear it?"

Anticipation filled the air as I eagerly awaited her solution. She moved to the back of the car, unfastened my overalls, slid them beneath my long-sleeve shirt, and secured them back in place. In that moment, a transformation occurred, and I felt instantly matured.

That day taught me two valuable lessons. Firstly, I realized that my mom respected me even when she didn't fully comprehend my actions. Something I consider when reflecting on my own students' behaviour and my response. Secondly, man, could that woman think on her feet. Another factor I consider in my own teaching.

# THAT'S NOT WHAT THIS BOOK IS ABOUT. IT'S REALLY ABOUT THIS:

As educators, we anticipate moments of transformation. We acknowledge, even if we may not always embrace it, that school serves as a platform for children to evolve, experiment with new friendships, clothing choices, and concepts. It's not always a smooth journey; in fact, the more observant we are, the more we recognize that amidst lessons on historical events like the War of 1812, our students may be grappling with internal struggles that are entirely unfamiliar to us. Funny, I was never really trained for this part of the job. Teacher's

# THAT'S NOT WHAT THIS BOOK IS ABOUT

College skipped right over developmental psychology, significant mental health battles, learning differences, the teen individuation process and decided to do three weeks on fake classroom management scenarios and marking schemes. I will let you decide which category should have been allotted more focus.

As I write this, I'm rewatching "Alien" for the 345th time, a film I always had playing in the background while working on major academic papers throughout university. Not sure if it fits the topic, but let's see how it goes as I type. On a random note - why do you think Ash tries to attack Ripley with that rolled-up magazine? There must have been simpler and faster methods available - it always struck me as an unusual choice. One life lesson from this movie could be the importance of staying vigilant and adaptable in the face of the unknown. Just as the characters in the film had to navigate a terrifying and unpredictable situation, we too may encounter challenges that require quick thinking, resourcefulness, and courage to overcome obstacles like getting me into daycare dressed in baby overalls. This movie serves as a reminder to always be prepared for the unexpected and to remain resilient in the face of adversity. OK focus, Jo!

I teach a Grade 12 course called "Challenge and Change in Society," which covers a wide range of important topics including psychology, psychological development, socialization, stereotypes, and oppression. It's a course that encourages critical thinking and discussion on key societal issues. I always find it fascinating that when we explore the concept of teenagers individuating and forming their identities, followed by an in-depth discussion on socialization and indoctrination within school and society, students sometimes struggle to fully engage with these ideas. By the time a 17-year-old student joins my class, it often feels like the process has already unfolded without them fully realizing it.

First, we delve into the various aspects of socialization - examining how family, school, friends, media, culture, and religion shape our identities, thoughts, responses, and behaviours. We explore the significant influence these factors have on shaping who we are. Next, we transition into discussing Erikson's psychosocial development stages, focusing on how teenagers navigate the formation of their identities. We explore strategies for teens to develop strong and authentic identities, rather than being plagued by identity confusion throughout their lives. Erik Erikson's psychosocial development theory outlines eight stages of human development, each characterized by a unique psychosocial crisis that individuals must navigate to achieve healthy psychological growth. The first stage, Trust vs. Mistrust, occurs in infancy, where the primary task is to develop a sense of trust in the world. This is followed by Autonomy vs. Shame and Doubt in toddlerhood, where children strive to assert their independence while learning to balance it with societal expectations. The stages progress through childhood, adolescence, and adulthood, addressing challenges such as Identity vs. Role Confusion, Intimacy vs. Isolation, and Generatively vs. Stagnation. Each stage presents opportunities for personal growth and self-discovery, ultimately culminating in the final stage of Integrity vs. Despair in old age, where individuals reflect on their lives and come to terms with their accomplishments and regrets. Erikson's theory emphasizes the importance of successfully navigating these stages to achieve a sense of fulfillment and wholeness throughout the lifespan.

Consider this: as a society, we often dictate to children who they should be, how they should present themselves, and even how they should communicate, long before we encourage them to develop their own unique and self-directed identities. How can we provide unwavering support for the former and then expect the latter to naturally emerge? How do we influence and guide children extensively, only to become frustrated when they show signs of being easily influenced by external factors? These are thought-provoking questions that prompt us to reflect on the complexities of nurturing individuality and independence in young minds. Why do we shove all of these preconceived notions filled with stereotypes and prejudice and then expect them to take on the world at face value? And even more importantly, how do I help create a space and an educational model that allows those very students and the environment to change, to grow and to become free of those constraints? If you find that concept bewildering, consider this: we then place the expectation on these 17-year-old individuals to have a clear vision of what they want to pursue for the entirety of their lives. They are tasked with selecting classes, extracurricular activities, clubs, and universities that are meant to intricately shape their future paths.

There is a certain simplicity in selecting an outfit. Deciding what to wear, when to wear it, choosing colour combinations, considering fabric content, selecting the right shoes, and even deciding on a hairstyle - all these elements hold significance because they serve as a visual representation of who we are or who we aspire to be in that particular moment. Our clothing choices can convey a lot about our identity and personal style, making them a powerful form of self-expression. It's true that we often tend to pigeonhole individuals based on the outfit they wore on the first day of school, associating them with a particular image or identity. This can create challenges for teenagers who may feel pressured to maintain that initial perception, despite their desire for change or growth. The expectations from friends, teachers, and family members can make it difficult for them to metaphorically "change outfits" and explore different aspects of themselves. Creating a supportive environment for teenagers isn't just about allowing them to be themselves; it's about providing a space where they can freely explore and evolve into whoever they aspire to be, in all their different forms. It's a journey of self-discovery and growth, where they can embrace various identities and possibilities as they navigate through the process of becoming. And some day, I can assure you, they will want their overalls back again.

# CLASS IS IN SESSION

## FEATURED VIDEO

# 3

# DRAWING AN OVAL &
# POWER OF ART

Uncle Ray, even though I rarely address him by that title, has been the most incredible combination of older brother, father figure, and uncle one could ever hope for. But shh, let's keep this praise between us to ensure he stays grounded and humble. Let me tell you a little about Ray, before we jump into the lesson I never knew I needed. Ray isn't too much older than me considering he is my uncle by definition. Ray was only 13 the year I was born and he always had a knack for teaching and learning, particularly in physics. I have to imagine Ray's career as an educator is what kept him so youthful. His quick wit and charm often commands the room over his physical size, standing at 5'8. Ray reminds me of an older Ryan Reynolds with short, salt and peppered hair. His charismatic smile and quick wit are reminiscent of the beloved actor, but Ray's own unique charm shines through in his thoughtful gestures and genuine kindness. Just like Reynolds, Ray has a way of lighting up a room with his presence and making everyone feel at ease with his easy going nature. At least, that's how I imagine Ryan Reynolds to be. P.S. You're welcome from Canada for Ryan Reynolds, as well as Uncle Ray.

One time, Ray had me sit in a chair (a red pleather one to be exact, from a time long passed) as a form of punishment. I ended up doodling all over it while my mom was catching up on sleep due to her night shifts as a nurse. It was a memorable moment that we can look back on now with a mix of amusement and nostalgia. My time in "confinement" didn't last long, as I managed to sneak upstairs without Ray noticing, wake up my mom, and share the whole "injustice" with her. Ray also taught me how to dance to Hall and Oates in front of the mirror in my mom's room. On any given day filled with laughter and music, Ray would patiently show me the steps and encourage me to let go of any self-consciousness. With each beat of the music, we twirled and grooved, creating our own little dance routine that brought joy and spontaneity into an otherwise ordinary day. Ray's infectious energy and enthusiasm were contagious, and that made him a great teacher. Often we were both lost in the music, moving in sync and reveling in the simple pleasure of dancing like nobody was watching. His talent as a physics teacher was truly remarkable, and witnessing him inspire and engage high school students served as the foundation of my own journey towards becoming an educator. Ray's influence and teaching style have left a lasting impact on me.

At the ripe old age of seven (yes, just seven years old), we all gathered to watch Stephen King's "The Thing" one late Saturday afternoon after a banger of a dance session. I bravely faced the movie like a champ, continued with the rest of the evening, and prepared for bed as usual, with a slight terror in my mind. As I approached my bed and pulled back the covers, my mischievous uncle, who had been hiding under the bed for what seemed like hours, suddenly reached out and grabbed my ankles! I let out a startled yelp, a mixture of surprise and amusement, as he emerged from his hiding spot with a wide grin on his face. His playful antics never failed to catch me off guard, but they always brought a sense of lighthearted fun to our time together. As I tried to catch my breath from the sudden scare, Ray chuckled and teased me about falling for this classic prank. Despite the initial shock, I couldn't help but laugh along with him, appreciating the spontaneous and playful spirit that he always brought into our interactions. It was a playful scare that left quite an impression, to say the least. I did indeed leave him some rather angry "fan mail" on his pillow at some point as a form of retaliation. I'm not entirely sure what pushed me over the edge, but after the ankle grabbing incident, I felt we were even. However, let's not get sidetracked further by these playful antics. Let's refocus and move on to the main theme of this chapter: Ray's passion for art.

Ray is not only an amazing artist but also had one of the most impressive comic book collections I've ever come across. As a child born in the 1960s, he immersed himself in the colourful world of superheroes and villains, collecting rare editions and original artwork that showcased his deep appreciation for the art form. However, if you ever have the pleasure of meeting him, it's best not to bring up the topic. He still has regret over the day he made the decision to sell off the entire collection for reasons that may seem insane to us now. Perhaps it was a reflection of the era, as the Baby Boomer generation parted ways with their cherished childhood comics and sports card collections in anticipation of the looming Y2K bug in 1999. As the clock ticked closer to the turn of the millennium, a sense of uncertainty gripped the world. The Y2K bug, a digital spectre looming over the horizon, threatened to disrupt the very fabric of modern society. With fears of widespread computer malfunctions and chaos abound, individuals and organizations scrambled to fortify their systems against the impending technological apocalypse. As the countdown to the year 2000 began, the world held its breath, waiting to see if the Y2K bug would unleash its havoc or if humanity's resilience would prevail in the face of this unprecedented challenge. However, what an anti-climactic event that turned out to be! Now, let's get back to Ray.

Selling his collection of comics is a bittersweet memory for him, but his artistic talents and passion for comics remain a cherished part of his identity. Not only did he have a deep love for comics, particularly Marvel (though I still stand by my superhero pick - Superman), but he would also create his own drawings of these beloved characters. Ray's artistic talents extended beyond just admiring comics; he brought these characters to life through his own creative interpretations. It's truly inspiring to see someone so passionate about a form of art that they actively contribute to it themselves. He would often spend hours in his comic room meticulously recreating the elaborate covers of his favourite issues. I was always in awe of his talent, the precision, and the calm focus he displayed while drawing these incredible pieces. I don't think he ever fully realized just how much his artistry impressed me. I suppose this section will serve as a test to see if he reads this book in its entirety and discovers the admiration and appreciation I hold for his creative skills. Love you, Ray!

I wanted to follow in Ray's artistic footsteps, so I approached him and asked if he could teach me how to draw. We sat together at his drafting table, a piece of furniture I admired for its size and its role in producing such amazing art, and began with the basics - drawing an oval. It was a simple yet significant starting point in my journey to explore the world of art under Ray's guidance. In just a matter of minutes, Ray effortlessly sketched an oval on the page before us, displaying the perfect blend of skill and casual ease that only a true artist possesses. This oval was unmistakably Ray's signature touch. P.S. I actually had Ray draw this for my book to ensure authenticity. It's amazing how a simple shape drawn by a skilled hand can hold so much meaning and significance in our artistic journey together.

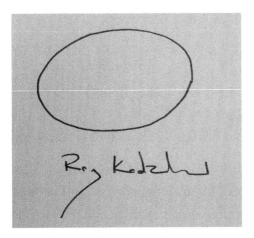

As it was my turn, I picked up the pencil, feeling a mix of excitement and nervousness. I studied Ray's perfectly drawn oval, then glanced at the blank page in front of me. Ensuring my pencil was sharpened to match his precise tool, I took a moment to gather my thoughts. This was the beginning of a creative journey, and I was eager to see where it would lead. I gazed at the comic book re-creation on the wall behind him, drawing inspiration from the colourful and dynamic world of superheroes. Then, I turned my attention back to Ray's oval, studying its shape and proportions once more. With a tiny bead of sweat trickling down the right side of my brow, I took a deep breath, ready to pour all my focus and dedication into the task ahead. For the next five minutes, I meticulously mimicked his oval, each stroke bringing me closer to capturing the essence of his artistic style. And with that, I proudly presented my own rendition of the masterpiece, a small yet significant step in my artistic journey.

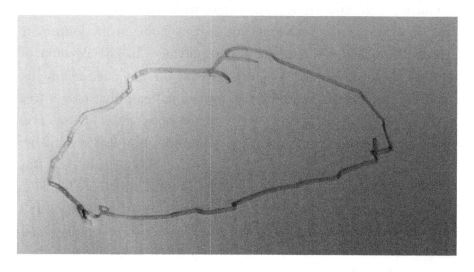

I looked at the finished product in horror and quickly erased it. Ray looked at me and said, "Don't worry about it being perfect. The oval is supposed to be imperfect, just to give you a starting point."

Imperfect? Was he crazy? Did he not understand how much I wanted to excel in drawing? If I started my artistic journey with a flawed oval, how could I ever hope to create masterpieces like the ones hanging within my view?  So, once more, I focused intently on his oval and made another attempt. This time, I dialled up my concentration even further, striving for perfection with every stroke. It was at that moment I made a conscious decision to apply a firmer grip and increased pressure, believing it would bring me closer to achieving my ideal oval. I was so engrossed in the process that I'm certain my fingertips went numb from the intense effort during this particular attempt.

Once more, I looked down in disgust, realizing that this oval could not be erased. In fact, it seemed to be permanently etched into the desk beneath it. Frustrated, I knew that this flawed oval needed to be banished from existence. With determination, I crumpled the sheet of blank paper in my fist, ensuring that this imperfect creation would never see the light of day again. I looked at Ray, and he gazed back at me, saying, "Again." Feeling a mix of determination and frustration, I embarked on another attempt over the next 20 minutes, a timeframe often considered crucial in assessing one's artistic potential. However, as the minutes ticked by, I found myself growing increasingly disheartened. Eventually, I made the difficult decision to abruptly give up on perfecting the oval. I abandoned my artistic pursuits and didn't

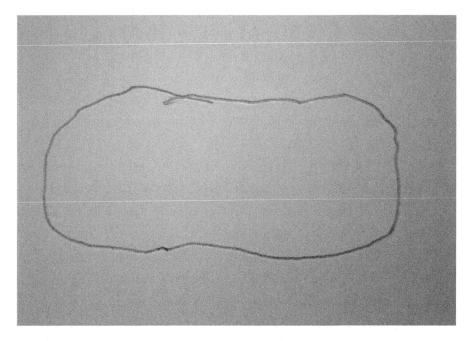

pick up a pencil again for two decades, until I found myself in a different role as a teacher. It was a surprising turn of events, and I'm not entirely sure what prompted me to give drawing another chance after all those years. But here's the story of how I rediscovered my passion for art.

# THAT'S NOT WHAT THIS BOOK IS ABOUT. IT'S REALLY ABOUT THIS:

A few years into my 22-year teaching career, I found myself picking up that pencil once more. I can't pinpoint the exact moment that spurred me to do so. Perhaps I was simply seeking a way to quiet my mind that didn't involve watching reruns of "Buffy the Vampire Slayer." It could have been the influence of the children I was surrounded by every day. They were constantly trying new things - some challenging, some enjoyable, and some downright scary - yet they faced them head-on regardless. Their fearless approach to exploration may have inspired me to revisit my own creative pursuits.

I introduced art into my classes to capture the attention of students who might not typically engage with topics like politics, world history, or the electoral system. While my initial intention was to offer a reprieve from traditional academics, I discovered something far more meaningful. It was like stumbling upon a touch of magic. Oh, but I'm getting ahead of myself. Back to the drawing board.

When faced with this unusual yet inspiring revelation that I wanted to draw, my first instinct was to go shopping. But not just any shopping - I didn't head to Walmart or Staples like most people would. Instead, I made a beeline for the local arts store in downtown Toronto near my house. I don't even think Michaels existed back then! If I was going to pursue art, I figured I needed top-notch equipment. Well, who am I kidding? I just really enjoyed shopping!

Off I went to Above Ground Art Supplies. I carefully selected the perfect pencils (blue Staedtler, to be exact), a matching blue pencil sharpener, and a white eraser with blue packaging (also Staedtler, naturally). Next, I browsed the sketchbooks and settled on one with thick pages and large rings, ensuring the cover would wrap around the entire book. With my supplies in hand, I felt ready to dive into my artistic journey.

As I gazed at the blank page, surprisingly, I didn't immediately attempt an oval. Instead, a memory from a Grade 9 class I once visited at school resurfaced. The students were using a grid system to section off images and then recreating them in their sketchbooks using the same grid system. Was this considered art? Was it cheating? I wasn't sure, but I decided to give it a try anyway.

My initial attempt was a disaster! I mean, even a 10 year old could have done better. I attempted to recreate a Spiderman cover, but it turned into a tangled mess. So, I tore it out and began anew. The second attempt still fell short, but I discovered that drawing the grid itself was oddly soothing, so that was a small consolation. Page after page was ripped from the rings, one after another, and then 17 more times.

One might assume that these setbacks would discourage me, especially considering how easily an oval had defeated me in my younger days. Surprisingly, it had the opposite effect. The less I focused on perfection, the more the image improved. When I released the pressure to make it look good, the lines became clearer. I was doing this solely for myself, in the peaceful ambiance of my home, with Buffy reruns flickering in the background. It turned into a calming and relaxing experience. One valuable life lesson we can learn from Buffy the Vampire Slayer is the importance of embracing your inner strength and resilience, even in the face of adversity. Just like Buffy, we all have the power within us to overcome challenges, fight our own battles, and stand up for what we believe in. It teaches us that we can find courage, friendship, and purpose in the most unexpected places, and that we are capable of facing our fears and emerging stronger on the other side.

Reflecting on my past struggles with that elusive oval, I had a profound realization that many people never grasp: the relentless pursuit of perfection can hinder you from achieving remarkable feats if you allow it to. The demand for flawlessness can trick you into believing you're not capable before you even give yourself a chance to grow. And then, it hit me - I was a teacher. By releasing the grip of perfection, I discovered the true essence of art. Letting go of the need

for symmetry brought me tranquility. Embracing "not so bad" instead of striving for greatness brought me contentment. Shedding expectations revealed my boundless potential. As I honed my skills, I started drawing superheroes for my students, framing them, and gifting them as tokens of inspiration for the incredible individuals they were.

Integrating art into my teaching wasn't just about inclusivity, although it did achieve that. It was about encouraging my students to venture into uncharted territories and attempt things they never thought possible. How can I guide my students in releasing the grip of perfectionism? How do I teach them to relax their grip on the pencil while sketching that elusive oval? How can I persuade them that perfection is a mirage, one that constrains their true potential for greatness? These are the questions that drive me as an educator. So, I incorporated it all. Imagine giant collages made from political magazines, filled with headlines, campaign slogans, and reflections of political victories and setbacks. Picture a canvas spanning over 6 desks pushed together, with the entire class collaborating on it. As they worked together, they would engage in conversations about current issues and the elements they incorporated into the collage. Debates, discussions, and creativity would intertwine seamlessly in this dynamic learning experience. We transformed entire walls at Metro Prep Academy by crafting a stencil of the iconic Mona Lisa. Projecting it onto a massive 15-foot wall, we meticulously painted and adorned it with various pieces from Da Vinci's repertoire. Throughout this creative process, we delved into discussions about the profound influence this multifaceted genius - artist, scientist, mathematician, and inventor - had on his era and continues to have on our world today.

I have expanded my art projects to involve the entire school community. When students are not in my classes, I bring my classes to them. One of the most remarkable projects we undertook was on Truth and Reconciliation Day. Thousands of puzzle pieces were painted orange, forming a loose canvas measuring 10 feet in length and 4 feet in width. This setup allowed the entire school to take turns piecing together their contributions to create a powerful final image. Truth and Reconciliation Day is a day dedicated to acknowledging and honouring the experiences of Indigenous People, particularly in the context of colonialism and the impact of residential schools. It serves as a time for reflection, education, and healing, aiming to promote understanding, empathy, and reconciliation between Indigenous and non-Indigenous communities. The day provides an opportunity to recognize historical injustices, foster dialogue, and work towards building a more inclusive and equitable society. We stencilled and painted TRUTH on the canvas and proceeded to try to reassemble these puzzle pieces. In our art project, when we encountered challenges that seemed insurmountable, we stumbled upon a profound metaphor for the losses endured during the cultural genocide - the realization that some pieces may never be fully restored. However, it is our responsibility to listen, to make sincere efforts, and to create space for Indigenous communities to reconstruct in ways that honour their needs and aspirations. The conversations that emerged from this experience were nothing short of beautiful and enlightening, showcasing a deep understanding of the harm inflicted and a shared vision for a hopeful future.

The oval was never the issue. It was always about the mindset. To empower children to achieve great things, it's crucial for them to understand that it's perfectly fine to make mistakes, to struggle, and to not excel at everything right away. The key is to embrace failure as a stepping stone to success, to persevere through challenges, and to keep trying without giving up. It's all about fostering a growth mindset that encourages resilience, learning from setbacks, and continuous improvement. It's common for individuals to withdraw from classes due to self-doubt about their abilities, fear of not achieving top grades, or the perception that the subject doesn't align with their future goals. It's regrettable that we often criticize them when they struggle in a class. But why should we do that? I believe that true education goes beyond excelling only in areas where we are naturally talented. It's about embracing challenges, trying new things, and putting in the effort to improve even in areas where we may struggle initially. Education is a journey of growth, learning, and pushing ourselves to become better versions of ourselves, even if it means "sucking a little less" along the way.

## CLASS IS IN SESSION

### FEATURED VIDEO

# NURSED INTO
# HEALTH & BECOMING

I spent my childhood at Wellesley Hospital in downtown Toronto. It wasn't because I was unwell, but because my mother was a nurse, and back in those days, it was common practice to bring your child to work. The hospital had some relaxed rules, like smoking being allowed in patients' rooms, which may not align with today's standards. It was within the walls of that hospital that I took my very first steps towards my mother's head nurse, Mrs. Lichacz. Mrs. Lichacz was tough, fair and brilliant. You could hear and feel her laughter echo through the halls like thunder rumbling on a rainy spring day. Those initial steps in that hospital marked the beginning of a journey that would ultimately transform everything for me.

My mother worked on the Plastics and Ear, Nose, and Throat (ENT) floor of the hospital, which meant that my first glimpses into the world were through the eyes of burn victims and my first sounds were of a laryngectomy patient learning to communicate once more. These experiences provided me with a unique perspective on life and instilled in me a deep sense of empathy and understanding for those facing challenges and adversity. As my mother made her rounds, she would introduce me to patients on the Plastics and ENT floor. I would walk around, distribute lunch menus, and engage in conversations with patients and their families. One day, a laryngectomy patient arrived on the floor. My mom explained that she had undergone surgery to remove her voice box due to cancer and was now in the hospital to recover. Despite being exposed to terms like cancer and seeing patients with surgical openings in their necks, I never felt fear within those hospital halls. It was a place where compassion and understanding prevailed, shaping my perspective on health and humanity. When I was around 6 years old, I entered that patient's room as she pressed the buzzer for assistance. Before my mom could arrive, I noticed that the patient was pointing to her throat, where some blood and secretions had leaked outside of the tube inserted in her neck. One might expect that I would have been terrified, screamed, or fled the room never to return. In that moment, instead of being scared, I calmly entered the patient's room, observed the situation, and assured her that I would fetch my mother to help. I stayed by her side as my mom addressed the issue, and in that process, I learned how to communicate effectively with someone who couldn't speak. This experience fostered a sense of connection and resilience within me. It was a powerful moment that showed me I could rely on my mom to solve almost any problem, and I stood by her side as she cared for and healed those in need.

On the Plastics floor, I encountered severe burn victims, including a man undergoing extensive grafts on his face and body to recover from a devastating fire. As I wandered the halls, I befriended this older gentleman. My mother introduced me to him, and I observed his heavily scarred face, understanding the trauma he had endured as my mom always took the time to explain the circumstances to me. Instead of being frightened by the scars he bore, I was drawn to the shiny appearance of his fingers. Curious, I inquired about it, and he promptly shared how the fire had altered the appearance of his hands, making them shiny. He reassured me that they no longer caused him pain; they would just always look that way. This simple exchange shifted my perspective, enabling me to see the person beyond the physical damage. I learned to see someone's inner strength and resilience, recognizing that true beauty lies not in perfection, but in the courage to face adversity with grace and determination.

The lasting impact that stays with me to this day wasn't physical damage; it was something unseen. I recall a man sitting alone in a room that was strictly off-limits to me. I could only hand him his menu, discuss his situation briefly, but forming a friendship was out of the question. This room was not just restricted to me; even the staff were barred unless they were in full protective gear, akin to a hazmat suit. He had no visitors, no family, no friends. Occasionally, as I passed by his room, I would glance through the small window in his door and a sense of sadness would wash over me. It wasn't just a thought; it was a deep feeling of empathy that resonated within me. This was perhaps the first time I truly experienced such a profound level of empathy. It pained me to see him gazing out the window, appearing calm yet undeniably alone. What I didn't realize at that time was that he was battling AIDS. The fear surrounding the disease prevented anyone from entering his room, touching him, or offering him comfort. It was as if he had been abandoned long before he passed away, left to face his struggles alone. Back then, I couldn't comprehend why we weren't allowed to go in, but even as a 10-year-old, I could grasp that the true harm inflicted upon that man wasn't just the disease itself but the sense of being erased from human connection. I often wonder if my occasional waves through the window brought him any comfort or only served as a painful reminder of his isolation.

Within these hospital halls, seemingly simple questions often unveiled profound answers. Whenever we encountered her colleagues, my mom would introduce me to all the doctors and nurses she worked alongside. One day, she introduced me to Rick. As he knelt down and shook my hand, my mom praised him as one of the finest nurses she had ever worked with, setting the stage for a memorable conversation.

I gazed at him, my brow furrowed in confusion, and blurted out, "I didn't know boys could be nurses!" Without hesitation, Rick responded, "Joanna, you can be anything you want to be." To which I quipped, "Even a butterfly?" Rick affirmed, "Even a butterfly." While I may not have pursued my childhood dream of flight beyond that moment, his empowering words have remained a fundamental part of my identity.

# THAT'S NOT WHAT THIS BOOK IS ABOUT. IT'S REALLY ABOUT THIS:

It does seem like I was on the path to becoming a nurse, doesn't it? However, handling blood in an emergency only to faint afterward isn't exactly a solid foundation for a career in medicine. So, did growing up in a hospital influence my choice to become a biology teacher? Or did I dive into the realm of chemistry?

Chemistry wasn't my calling, but let me share a little side story about my chemistry experience. In Grade 13, back when we had Ontario Academic Credit (OAC) in high school, I watched "Free Willy" and had a total change of heart about my future aspirations. I was so captivated by the movie that I decided to ditch all my previous plans and pursue a career as a marine biologist. I selected Simon Fraser University in British Columbia for its supposed proximity to the ocean, only to discover it was actually situated 3000 feet up a mountain in the interior of the province. Nevertheless, upon arrival, I managed to secure a spot on the varsity volleyball team, skipped the biology lab entirely, and relied on multiple-choice guesswork to scrape by with a 65% in chemistry. I struggled to grasp the concept of a "mole." In chemistry, a mole is a unit of measurement used to express the amount of a substance. One mole of a substance contains Avogadro's number of particles, which is approximately $6.022 \times 10^{23}$ particles. This unit is commonly used in chemical calculations to determine the number of atoms, molecules, or ions in a given sample of a substance. It's like saying "a dozen eggs" but for particles. Piece of cake, right? My coach arranged a tutor for me, who unfortunately ended up hitting on me and couldn't effectively explain the concept either. I even failed to remove the cellophane from my chemistry textbook to try and figure out the mole on my own. To top it off, I witnessed a classmate getting caught cheating on the chemistry final, likely because he too couldn't wrap his head around the mole concept. Feeling defeated, I reached out to my mom and confessed my struggles with science, my doubts about pursuing marine biology, and my overall uncertainty about succeeding in university. To my surprise, she didn't judge or make me feel guilty for wanting to quit. Instead, she showed understanding and compassion by allowing me to take a break and go skiing at Whistler before returning home. And so, that's exactly what I did. Skiing in Whistler offers a serene escape into nature's snowy embrace, where the exhilarating rush down the slopes acts as a soothing balm for the soul, making it a perfect stress relief getaway - or a reason to avoid what was really happening.

Upon returning home, I found myself grappling with doubts about my ability to return to school. I questioned whether I even wanted to go back, if I could go back, or if I was capable enough to succeed. Throughout this tumultuous period of self-doubt and uncertainty, my mom remained a pillar of strength, offering silent support as I navigated this crisis of identity and confidence. Looking back, I realized that my poor grades were a direct result of one crucial factor - my work ethic, or lack thereof. I didn't put in the effort required, instead opting to pretend to work and then shifting blame onto my perceived lack of ability. It made me ponder how often we tend to find excuses for our shortcomings, attributing failures to aspects of our character rather than taking responsibility for them. That first year at university was undeniably a failure in my character. However, I did manage to enjoy a skiing trip in Whistler, so I suppose all's well that ends well. This reminds me of a surfing trip in Costa Rica. More on that later.

Miraculously, I found my way back to university, specifically the University of Western Ontario. My time as a student was not yet finished, nor was I ready to retire my school jersey. This time around, I made a conscious decision to pursue what I truly loved, rather than what I thought I should be or do. Inspired by my mom's career choices based on passion, I opted for courses that resonated with my heart. What set this new approach apart was my unwavering commitment to give my all to these courses of love. It wasn't a deliberate decision or a solemn vow; it simply became second nature to pour my heart and soul into my studies. During that transformative year, my mom would make the two and a half hour drive every other weekend to pick me up and take me back to school. Without fail, on each journey, she would ask me, "What did you learn in school?" And instead of the typical teenage response of "nothing," I found myself eagerly sharing my newfound knowledge and experiences with her. During those car rides, I took the opportunity to educate my mom on the political philosophies of Rousseau, Kant, Voltaire, Marx, and Plato. I shared my admiration for my political philosophy professor, Bob Melvin, who had a unique teaching style. Despite delving into profound philosophical concepts that underpin politics, Professor Melvin never once wrote anything on the board during his lectures. Professor Melvin's unconventional teaching methods included carrying a piece of chalk and sporadically jotting down a few words on the beige concrete walls or a random student's desk. This quirky approach led the entire class to eagerly stand up and strain their eyes to capture these profound insights. By the end of the semester, I had accumulated a grand total of only three pages of notes, a testament to the impact of his enigmatic teaching style. And as for the final exam question? It was so unexpected, you'll never believe it. Want to take a guess?

"You can lead a horse to water, but you can't make him think. Using three political theorists studied throughout this course, prove your thesis."

Can you believe it? I vividly recall the moment of panic as I glanced around the room, feeling the weight of 150 eyes on me, all of us bracing for what seemed like an inevitable failure. But then, something remarkable happened - we began to write. I began to write. And to my surprise, the words flowed from my mind as if I were an expert, as if I didn't need the notes because Bob had taught me how to learn, not just memorize content. It was a true testament to the power of understanding over rote memorization and the test score results for that class would prove it. During all those journeys back home with my mom, I believe I learned how to teach - her inquisitive questions and Bob's unconventional teaching style both played a role in shaping my approach to education. It was a valuable lesson in communication and sharing knowledge that I carry with me to this day.

Stepping into my own classroom, ready to embark on my teaching journey, I never realized just how much I would draw upon my mom's influence. My mom possessed a unique blend of patience, empathy, and intelligence that made her patients feel both comfortable and empowered. Her work ethic was unparalleled, serving as a driving force that inspired me, even when I didn't consciously realize it. She commanded respect from all who entered her world, leaving an indelible mark on me as I ventured into the realm of education. Growing up, I had the privilege of witnessing my mom pursue her passion with unparalleled dedication and skill. Her work ethic was truly remarkable, setting a standard that few could match. Observing my mom's strength and proficiency in her chosen field had a profound impact on me - it reshaped my perspective on teaching and inspired me to strive for excellence in my own journey as an educator. As I ventured into the world of teaching, I crafted three essential rules that have guided me faithfully for the past 23 years. These principles have been the cornerstone of my approach to education, shaping my interactions with students and colleagues alike.

# NUMBER ONE: DON'T MAKE THEM READ OUT LOUD (EMPATHY)

My mom, despite being an incredibly shy child - painfully so, as she would often recount - found her true strength and courage only after her divorce from my dad. It was during this period of devastation that she discovered a resilience within herself that she never knew existed. It's fascinating how adversity can sometimes be the catalyst for inner growth and empowerment, isn't it? My mom would share with me the harrowing tales of her school days, how she would feign illness to avoid facing her fears, and how her lack of confidence made her feel inadequate in the eyes of others. Reading aloud wasn't just a simple task for my mom - it symbolized pushing students out of their comfort zones, confronting their fears, and overcoming feelings of inadequacy before the real learning could begin. When I stepped into the role of a teacher, I made a conscious decision not to replicate that experience for my students. Was I flawless in my approach? Far from it. Allow me to share a story that highlights just how imperfect I was in my early days as a novice teacher.

About six years into my teaching career, I faced a significant challenge - a "Houston, we have a problem" moment, as they say in reference to Apollo 11. During every midterm, I conduct an in-class essay for all politics students. This exercise serves two main purposes: firstly, it evaluates a student's analytical skills rather than their memorization abilities, as they are allowed to consult their notes during the task. Secondly, it offers insight into their independent capabilities, devoid of external assistance like parental guidance, support from siblings at university, or tutoring help - you catch my drift. The in-class essay spans a three-day process, during which I collect their work at the end of each period and return it the following day for them to continue their work. On the first day of class, let's call him "Justin" (a pseudonym I'll use to avoid repeating "my student" throughout this story), Justin spent the entire 70-minute period doing absolutely nothing. He barely glanced at his notes, didn't even bother to write his name, let alone begin outlining an essay. It was a challenging start, to say the least. P.S. I spelled "pseudonym" correctly without the aid of spell check (cue applause). Throughout the class, I made several attempts to guide Justin towards essay mode, ensuring he grasped the question at hand. Each time, he reassured me in his most positive tone, saying, "I'm organizing it all in my head, Jo. Don't worry, this is just my process for tackling an essay." His confidence in his approach made me hesitant to push him further at that moment. As a novice teacher, I acknowledge that I made mistakes, but the story must go on.

On the second day of writing, Justin did put pen to paper. Once again, I approached him to offer support and motivation, only to be shooed away with Justin assuring me that he was in the final stages of solidifying his opinion and strategy. He claimed his notes were organized and ready to go. Trusting his words, I refrained from pushing him further. Reflecting back, I realize that as a new teacher, I should have taken different actions - perhaps making him stay after school or going over the questions more thoroughly. These experiences taught me valuable lessons as a "baby teacher."

On the third day, Justin finally began writing his essay, about 20 minutes into the class. He skipped over the required outline but managed to complete a good chunk before the final bell rang, signalling the end of the period. As I went around collecting papers, Justin barely glanced up at me, muttering, "I'm going to need more time, just leave me alone." I tried to reason with Justin, reminding him that he had three days to work on his essay, which he didn't utilize, but he continued to ignore me. I emphasized the importance of submitting his paper, but he still disregarded my requests. Finally, I made it crystal clear that I would not be grading anything unless he handed in his paper at that moment. Justin lost his composure. He glared at me, rose from his seat, unleashed a tirade about my teaching, flipped his desk, hurled his chair, and stormed out of the classroom. I stood there momentarily, with concerned students checking on me, before I gathered myself and trailed after him to the principal's office. Wayne, our administrator, listened to my account of the situation and inquired whether I believed Justin should face suspension or expulsion. I responded with a firm "Neither." While I made it clear that Justin could not return to my classroom, I emphasized that simply keeping him at home or expelling him from school would not address the underlying issues he was facing.

Over the next few months, Justin avoided eye contact with me in the halls, kept his head down, and remained quiet in other classes. He seemed to simply exist in a state of quiet reserve. However, things took a turn during the final exam, which he completed under the supervision of another teacher. As I began grading his exam, I came across a simple note that had nothing to do with the political system of Brazil, sparking my curiosity. The note, paraphrased as I lost the torn-out piece of paper during the school move, conveyed the following sentiment:

"I apologize for my behaviour during your exam. I am truly sorry for what happened, and I don't understand why I acted that way. Thank you for allowing me to remain at Metro. I can't imagine what I would have done if I had been expelled. Thank you for giving me another chance."

In that moment, it dawned on me that "reading out loud" was not just a literal task but a metaphor for the deeper empathy I needed to cultivate. I understood that developing empathy for my students would be a complex and nuanced process. It became clear that truly comprehending students as they entered my classroom and as they evolved as individuals and learners would be the most challenging yet crucial aspect of my role as an educator. I want to clarify that I don't believe in shielding students from challenging tasks or situations that may intimidate them. Tasks like reading out loud or completing an essay are essential for their growth and development, and I cannot exempt them from these responsibilities. Instead, my role is to understand why they feel fearful and find ways to empower them to face those challenges head-on. My goal is to help them find their voice and build their confidence so that even when their voice trembles, they can read through it with strength and resilience.

# NUMBER TWO: NEVER SET THEM UP TO LIE (ACCOUNTABILITY)

The principle passed down through generations in my family is to never place a child in a situation where they feel compelled to lie in order to avoid consequences for their actions. When given the opportunity, individuals may resort to dishonesty to protect themselves. It's important not to give them the chance to disappoint you a second time. For instance, if a student skips your class, they should not be rewarded with an extended lunch break. If a student claims to be sick on a test day, they should not be excused from taking the test. If a student requests to use the bathroom but is found in the gym instead, there should be repercussions. If a student fails to submit an assignment on time or resorts to looking at their notes during a test, they should face the appropriate consequences. I refrain from asking direct accusatory questions like "Did you skip class?" or "Were you cheating on the test?" Instead, I focus on addressing the behaviour and its impact. In situations where I am aware that a student has made a mistake or done something they may regret and feel embarrassed about, I choose not to directly ask them about it. In such situations, I address the mistake as a fact and focus on finding solutions for restitution. I intervene if I sense they are about to offer a dishonest response, emphasizing that the mistake itself is not as detrimental as compounding it with a lie. At the beginning of each class, I set clear expectations: while I understand that mistakes happen, I do not tolerate or overlook lies used to conceal them. Ensuring accountability is a crucial aspect of teaching. It can be one of the most challenging parts of the job, and it's an area where I'm still working on improving.

The key is to establish consequences that are meaningful and directly related to the specific issue at hand. By setting clear expectations and outlining the repercussions for not meeting them, we can help students understand the importance of taking ownership of their actions. When a student fails to submit work on time, I assign them a longer task to complete. If a student performs poorly on a test due to lack of preparation, I lead the next study sessions with clear work expectations for each session. If a student skips class for an extended lunch break, they are required to make up for the lost time by completing work after school. It's important that consequences are proportionate to the infraction, ensuring they remain valuable for both the teacher and the student. P.S. If you're running late in the morning, bring me a double-double coffee from Tim Hortons. While it may seem like bribery, I see it as a way to teach the students about accountability and responsibility in the real world.

# NUMBER THREE: WORK ETHIC

Were you satisfied with a hard C? How much time did you dedicate to studying for that test? How many revisions did you make for your latest essay? How much effort did you put into refining your presentation? Whom did you seek out to review your research paper? How many sources did you consult when creating your outline? I pose these questions because while grades may be the measure by which we are evaluated in what seems like an objective world, it is the effort and dedication you put into achieving that grade that truly reflects your character and, ultimately, influences your future success. Firstly, it's important to acknowledge that all students face challenges in certain subject areas. However, some students may struggle in areas that are not traditionally valued as highly. For instance, a student who excels in math may avoid the French classroom altogether. A biology enthusiast might be quick to dismiss social sciences from their schedule. Similarly, a computer whiz may steer clear of the gym environment. It's essential to recognize and address these diverse interests and strengths among students. That's our first challenge right there. We seem to have moved away from ensuring that our students receive a well-rounded education. Instead, they are expected to independently navigate their futures and design their academic paths accordingly.

Is it really realistic to expect a Grade 10 student to narrow their focus so early on? It's important to consider the value of a broad and diverse education that allows students to explore various subjects and interests before making such significant decisions. It appears that there is a push for students to specialize, particularly in STEM programs. Courses in art, gym, music, and philosophy seem to have taken a backseat to subjects like math, Shakespeare, and chemistry. While the sciences are undoubtedly important, the question remains: Why not utilize high school as an opportunity to provide students with a well-rounded education while also instilling the understanding that overcoming challenges is essential for achieving success? It's crucial to strike a balance between academic rigor and a diverse educational experience that fosters resilience and growth. Oftentimes, students express disappointment when they receive a C on a test. My initial inquiry is always, "Was it a hard C?" In other words, did you give it your all in achieving that grade? Did you seek feedback by having someone proofread your essay? Did you invest time in revising your report? Did you attempt to teach the material to someone else, recognizing that teaching is a powerful way to solidify your own understanding? These questions aim to encourage reflection on the effort and strategies employed in the learning process. If the response to those inquiries is affirmative, indicating that you truly exerted your best effort, then you have earned what I call a "hard C," and I will celebrate your achievement with a parade in your honour. However, if you coasted through, disregarded deadlines, put in minimal effort, or neglected your responsibilities until the eleventh hour, then I must admit that I am not impressed by any grade you received, even if it's an A. Effort, dedication, and responsibility are key factors in determining the true value of your academic performance.

It's important to note that I am not the type of educator who will advocate for everyone to receive an A simply because they put in effort. That's not the message I aim to convey. Effort is indeed significant, as is the final output. I firmly believe that there are various paths to reach the same goal, but I am steadfast in maintaining the integrity of the standards we set. It's about recognizing the balance between effort, performance, and the standards we uphold in education. Encouraging more students to become well-rounded individuals would not only foster genuine growth among students but also highlight the universal truth that all individuals will face challenges and struggles at some point in their academic and professional journeys. It is through overcoming these obstacles that true greatness is cultivated. By promoting a holistic approach to education that values diverse skills and experiences, we can empower students to navigate challenges with resilience and determination, ultimately paving the way for their personal and academic growth.

# CLASS IS IN SESSION

## FEATURED VIDEO

# 5

# STITCHED "GIRL" &
# BE THE BALL

**I relocated to Mansfield,** Ontario when I was 7 years old. The
decision stemmed from my parents' divorce, my mom's need for a
break from the demands of nursing, and my grandparents' venture
into purchasing a general store in what was deemed the world's
smallest town, something you'd find on an episode of "Schitt's Creek."
Embracing change, family unity, mutual support, and the
entrepreneurial spirit, my mom decided to join in on the business
endeavour, ensuring that we could engage in more consistent family
arguments - all in good humour, of course.

# STITCHED "GIRL" & BE THE BALL

During my time in the countryside, I encountered a plethora of memorable experiences. From discovering snakes in the boiler room to stumbling upon a deceased rat in the crawl space beneath our century-old home, the adventures were certainly diverse. I also recall playful antics with my uncles, who mischievously arranged my Barbies in "suggestive" poses while I slept, leading to amusing discoveries in the morning. There was the "almost-kiss" encounter with Jeremy Taggart, who would later become the drummer for Our Lady Peace, in the garage behind the store. Additionally, a skiing mishap that initially seemed like a broken leg turned out to be a more comical incident caused by a hole created by my ski pole. Each of these anecdotes adds to the colourful tapestry of my time spent in Mansfield, Ontario, but I think I'll stick to what inspired me most. Baseball.

During my inaugural summer in Mansfield, I made the decision to delve into the world of baseball. The sport seemed like the perfect pastime in such a quaint town, and the convenience of being able to walk to the diamond certainly played a role in my choice. I vividly recall the glove that was purchased for me - a grey, suede Wilson model. I understand that many may argue that a sturdier leather is essential for a quality baseball glove, but hey, I was just seven years old! Cut me some slack – that suede glove was a breeze to break in and suited my needs perfectly at the time. I must admit, without boasting too much, that once I set foot on that field, my talent in baseball shone through. I excelled, and it was evident that I had a natural aptitude for the sport. However, the most intriguing aspect of this tale lies in the unique setup of our small town. In Mansfield, due to its size, both girls and boys were placed on the same team, and what's more, we played baseball - not softball. This unconventional arrangement added an extra layer of excitement and camaraderie to our games, breaking away from traditional gender norms in sports. As the season unfolded, my skills on the field, particularly as a back catcher, flourished. I not only excelled at catching and throwing out players at second base, but I also held the prestigious position of batting third in the lineup (feel free to draw your own conclusions there)! And here's a fun twist to the story - the pitcher on our team was none other than Jeremy Taggart, the same Jeremy Taggart from Our Lady Peace. Given that my skills were well recognized, I was frequently called up to the higher level to step in when needed. Despite being restricted to playing outfield due to competitors' demands, I made such remarkable catches and saves that they regretted imposing such limitations. This backstory sets the stage for what is about to unfold - so hold onto your horses! Consider this a small prequel to the exciting events that are about to transpire, akin to a narrative teaser without the presence of Anakin Skywalker.

At the age of 12, my mom made the decision to transition back to city life, craving the hustle and bustle of the hospital environment once more. As we settled back into urban living, I encountered a rather peculiar roadblock. Initially, I was denied entry onto the local baseball team, presenting an unexpected challenge upon our return to the city. This marked the beginning of a new chapter in my baseball journey, filled with twists and turns as I navigated through this unforeseen obstacle. I distinctly remember the frustrating response I received when I expressed interest in joining the local baseball team in Whitby. The officials bluntly stated, "Well, we have girls' softball here. Why doesn't she go play that? It doesn't make sense for her to play with the boys, and she won't be able to keep up." This discriminatory attitude was disheartening, especially in a house league where no tryouts were required, and everyone was supposed to be allowed to play. It became evident that gender bias was at play, highlighting the challenges faced by girls who aspired to participate in traditionally male-dominated sports. In the face of adversity, I decided to take matters into my own hands. I bravely tried out for the house league team, boldly stating that if my baseball skills weren't up to par, they could kick me out of the league. Determined to prove myself, I took to the field and showcased my abilities. To the surprise of many skeptics, including some of those old men, I not only held my own but excelled, outperforming most of my peers. Winning that bet, I earned my spot on the team. However, the challenges and obstacles I faced were far from over, setting the stage for the next chapter in my baseball journey.

Given my role as a back catcher, I had a unique vantage point on the field. In the initial days of the league, before my presence as the sole girl on the field became widely known, I operated under the radar. It was only a matter of time before my true identity was revealed, much to the surprise and astonishment of those around me. The realization that I was breaking barriers and challenging stereotypes added an extra layer of intrigue to my baseball journey. Clad in my back catcher gear - knee pads, chest protector, and helmet - I took my position on the field with confidence. With a strong throw to second base and a fearless demeanour, I stood my ground even when faced with opponents attempting to run me over at home plate. The intensity and thrill of those moments on the field added to the excitement of the game. And yes, I do have a side story to share about those experiences, but you'll have to wait a bit longer for me to finish this tale. Remember, good things come to those who wait - you can't rush a good story!

At the start of each game, I would confidently take my position behind the plate as the catcher. After a few pitches, I would step up to the plate and swing for the fences, setting the tone for the game. As the game progressed, I would even make my way to the mound to showcase my pitching skills. It was during these moments that my mom, who was diligently keeping score, began to overhear the whispers and murmurs from other parents in the bleachers. The intrigue and curiosity surrounding my versatile performance on the field added an extra layer of excitement to the games. Perhaps some eagle-eyed spectators caught a glimpse of my face, despite my short hair, or noticed a movement that seemed a tad too feminine for their expectations. It's also possible that my assertive voice, directing my teammates when needed, drew attention and raised eyebrows among the onlookers. These subtle cues and behaviours may have sparked speculation and whispers among the parents in the bleachers, adding an element of mystery and intrigue to my presence on the field. In that pivotal moment, my mom would catch wind of the murmurs and questions swirling around the bleachers: "Is that a girl out there? Is there really a girl in this league? When did she join? Why wasn't this brought to our attention earlier? Are you certain that's a girl playing alongside your son?" The sudden realization and subsequent inquiries from the surprised parents added a new layer of intrigue and curiosity to the unfolding events on the baseball field.

And it was always at that precise moment that my mom, with unwavering pride in her voice, would assert, "Yes, that is a girl. She is my daughter," before calmly returning to her duties of scorekeeping. Her steadfast support and declaration served as a powerful reminder that gender should never be a barrier to pursuing one's passion and excelling in sports.

To take matters into my own hands. I asked my mom to stitch "GIRL" in bold block letters on the thigh of my uniform. This proactive move was aimed at addressing the controversy head-on as soon as I began warming up my shoulder. I wanted to make a statement - to proudly declare my gender and showcase that a girl could be one of the top players in the league. It was a bold and empowering gesture to challenge stereotypes and show that talent knows no gender boundaries. I wanted to make a statement - to show them that a girl was the one who just struck out their son. I aimed to assert my presence and demonstrate that I belonged wherever my skills and passion took me. It was about breaking barriers, challenging perceptions, and proving that gender should never limit where one can excel. I wanted to inspire others to see beyond stereotypes and embrace the idea that talent and determination know no boundaries.

Now, here's where the story takes a twist. Remember that tale I mentioned earlier? Well, here it is. As soon as I boldly stitched those letters onto my uniform, I inadvertently painted a target on my back. Some opposing players, fuelled by a misguided sense of superiority and outdated beliefs, saw me as a threat. Their misguided actions and embarrassing display of misogyny came to the forefront as they tried to undermine my place in the league simply because of my gender. But little did they know, their actions only fuelled my determination to prove them wrong and show that skill and passion trump prejudice any day. And when their masculinity was at risk, they took to the one place they thought they had an advantage - their physicality.

It's important to note that the overwhelming majority of boys in the league showed me respect and treated me as a valued ball player. I want to give a special shoutout to Matt Anderson, the standout pitcher in the league. Standing tall at over six feet, with a powerful stride to the plate and a fastball that could make your hand sting, Matt exemplified sportsmanship and camaraderie. His support and recognition of my skills meant a lot and showcased the true spirit of sportsmanship and teamwork on the field. When Matt caught wind of even the slightest hint of disrespect toward my talent from his teammates, he took a stand. He halted the warm-up session and beckoned me over to catch for him. With unwavering determination, he unleashed his pitches with more power and precision than ever before, as I crouched behind the plate, ready to receive each throw. This powerful display of solidarity and support not only showcased his respect for my abilities but also sent a clear message that talent and dedication should always be celebrated, regardless of gender. After the intense pitching session, Matt made his way over to his team and delivered a powerful message:

"That ball player is one of the FEW players in this league that can actually handle my pitches, and until you can figure out how to be better than she is I expect you shut your mouth, practice harder and learn from her."

This heartfelt declaration not only highlighted his unwavering support for me but also emphasized the importance of humility, hard work, and learning from each other on the field. Our lifelong friendship and mutual respect shone brightly in that moment, reinforcing the true essence of sportsmanship and camaraderie.

An opposing player saw the "GIRL" stitched on my pants and made it his personal mission to chirp me throughout the entire game (chirp being Canadian slang for trash talk). Despite the lack of physical contact in baseball, things took a turn when this player hit a powerful line drive to right field, setting himself up for what seemed like an easy triple. As he rounded third base, I, too, saw the ball coming in from the outfield as clearly as he did. Under normal circumstances, any other player would have tagged up and settled for third base. But this player was determined to make a statement. As he rounded third base and spotted the throw heading towards home plate, he seized the moment to try to showcase why I didn't deserve to be in the league. With a steely resolve, he watched as I caught the ball, and instead of playing it safe, he put his head down and kicked into an even higher gear than before. In his mind, he may have thought, "This is my chance to show this girl why she doesn't belong in our league." With the ball securely in my glove, I braced myself, reinforcing my stance and gripping the glove tightly with my other hand to ensure that I wouldn't drop the ball upon impact. I was prepared. I was determined to take this hit head-on, not just to prove my worth and belonging in the league, but to demonstrate my resilience, skill, and ability to rise above any challenge thrown my way. In a moment of clarity, I realized that I didn't need to take the hit to prove my skill. Taking the hit would only demonstrate that I could play in a way that relied solely on brute force, lacking strategy and finesse. So, in the final seconds before he reached home plate, I made a split-second decision. I leaned to the left, strategically positioning the same stitched thigh that I'm sure he despised in his path. This move wasn't just about avoiding a collision; it was about showcasing my intelligence, agility, and ability to outsmart my opponents on the field. As he collided with my leg, I swiftly tagged him on the back of his head, sending him flying about five feet back towards the backstop fence that shielded our fans. The impact was enough to declare him out, but as fate would have it, karma worked swiftly that day. His collarbone bore the brunt of the collision, serving as a reminder of the consequences of underestimating opponents. I often wonder, even 25 years later, when the rain sets in and his shoulder aches, does he reflect on the girl he could never outmatch on the field?

# THAT'S NOT WHAT THIS BOOK IS ABOUT. IT'S REALLY ABOUT THIS:

Your whole life, you are going to be told who you are, what you can and can't do, and where you should be in this world. Secret - NO

ONE KNOWS ANYTHING. You would think this part would be about gender and the constraints put upon us due to the sex we are born with, and that part of the story. However, the world, your parents, your partner, and your teachers are all going to expect things from you based on presumptions, and it will be your job to either conform or risk having "GIRL" metaphorically stitched on your pants.

Let's address gender expectations and realities in schools and classrooms. Are there stereotypes for young boys and girls at school? Absolutely. Are they ingrained in our culture and society, influencing our educational models? Again, yes. Do you observe patterns that mirror these stereotypes? Of course. Stereotypical expectations hold significant influence. At times, you may feel the urge to defy them completely, while other times you may find yourself embodying them. And sometimes, you may feel unsure of where you stand or why you stand there. That, my friends, is high school. As a teacher, it can be challenging to navigate this terrain - how can I support a student in their journey of self-discovery when they are constantly pressured to conform to societal standards of value? Parents expect us teachers to nurture strong individuals who can resist peer pressure, unless the pressure is coming from the parents themselves, such as wanting their child to become a doctor, in which case I am expected to teach them to comply. Do you see the dilemma here?

Why do you think I needed to stitch "GIRL" into my baseball uniform? I ask because I've come a long way from that time. When someone asks me today, "Are you a boy or a girl?" I respond without hesitation, "You can call me whatever you want, just make sure to compliment my hair." Let's set that aside for a moment, as I believe the more crucial part of the story is when I stepped aside while that player took it upon himself to teach me a lesson. As a teacher, my role is to guide students in recognizing when they need to step back and metaphorically tag the player on the back of their head. I know, I know, that metaphor did get a bit tangled in the weeds... even for me. Stay with me, maybe grab a cup of coffee to keep up the energy! Leaning out from the plate during that game wasn't an admission of inadequacy; it was a realization of my own strength and skill. Do you understand that? As a teacher, my role is to discover in what ways each student excels, because they all have unique strengths waiting to be uncovered. Now, how in the hell do I get around all the insecurities of those teen years to help them find out who they are and how strong they can be?

I joke, use sarcasm, and even bribe them with PS5s. I take them shopping at Yorkdale Mall and to Niagara Falls for an end-of-the-year class trip. I encourage them to speak freely and have their own opinions. I sneak them donuts, speak to their parents consistently and honestly. I never lie to them or hide anything from them or their parents. I cultivate relationships with my students that enable them to express their true selves, creating a safe space for self-discovery and growth. My goal is not just to empower them, but to establish a foundation of trust so that when I challenge them, they have faith in me and my guidance. When I engage in difficult conversations with them, they don't fear me. And when I affirm their power, they trust my words. This is the essence of why I teach. History class serves as the vehicle to reach that goal. History may be the subject, but empowering students is the ultimate objective.

# CLASS IS IN SESSION

## FEATURED VIDEO

# 6

# POST IT & ALL HEART

**Playing for the Senior** Girls' Volleyball Team under Gord Williamson at Anderson CVI was the ultimate honour. They were renowned as the best team, with a reputation that everyone recognized. My high school was dominated by volleyball, and being part of that team was a coveted dream for all. I aspired to join them, but I was clueless about how to make that dream a reality. Here's the issue: during my Grade 10 year, I spent half the season on the bench (either because the coach didn't like me or because I was a mouthy kid, one of the two). So, when Gord Williamson walked into our final tournament to assess our performance and select players for the Senior Volleyball Team (yes, I meant to capitalize that), I found myself sitting just four feet away from my coach, perched on the edge of the bench. At that moment, I assumed my volleyball career was over. So, I did what any half-decent athlete would do in my situation - I started playing rugby.

Rugby introduced me to a new realm with different coaches and a distinct atmosphere. It marked the inception of Anderson's girls' rugby team, and I approached the game with a fearlessness born from never experiencing injury before. What I found intriguing about rugby is that initially, greatness isn't a prerequisite; all that's required is unwavering dedication and giving it your all. Greatness will come in due time. Although I did end up breaking my collarbone at the end of that season, that's not the focus of this story (a curious throwback to my baseball days, isn't it?). It wasn't the game of rugby itself that would alter the trajectory of my life; rather, it was the perception of my play by that *one* coach that would open the door to an opportunity I didn't even realize was within reach.

Fast forward to the next volleyball season (Grade 11). I had nearly abandoned my aspirations of making the senior team, despite having the potential for three more years on the team (as high school in Ontario extended to Grade 13 at that time). I had reluctantly accepted the idea of enduring another year of junior volleyball under the coach who seemed to dislike me. And then, the most unexpected turn of events occurred - a moment of fate, kismet, serendipity (by the way, "Serendipity" was a great movie with John Cusack). Gord Williamson extended a *personal invitation* for me to attend tryouts for the Senior Volleyball Team (yes, I'm still capitalizing it). Prompting the question, "Why would you invite me to try out when you've never seen me play? When I spent the majority of last season sitting on the bench?" Gord responded with these words: "Hussey (assistant coach) mentioned that you approached rugby with unparalleled heart and determination, surpassing any athlete he's encountered. Skill can always be improved, but one's heart and drive are innate. So, I'm willing to bet that giving you a chance will validate his assessment."

Is he serious? How do I dive into this tryout? Am I truly capable? I feel like I'm on the verge of a panic attack. All of those thoughts raced through my mind, but somehow I managed to focus on what was necessary. I grabbed my volleyball shoes, adorned my lucky "Beauty and the Beast" band aid across my thigh (a quirky ritual of mine, don't ask), and stepped onto the court, fully aware of my lack of experience. Despite my determination, I realized that these girls were far superior players than I was on that particular day. Tryouts went on throughout the week.

Have you ever tried pushing a piece of lumber? Gord had a unique way of starting each practice. He would wrap a two foot long 2x4 in a towel, and we would push it up and down the volleyball court until our quads, hamstrings, and glutes ached so intensely that lying down on our stomachs was the only way to find relief from the immense pain. When it came to volleyball, I threw myself for every ball, pushed myself to the limit, absorbed every instruction eagerly, served with all my might, and always led the pack in every drill our coach threw at us.

On the last day of tryouts, the final team roster was set to be posted outside the gym, revealing who needed to attend the 7 am practice the next day. The dilemma was that I had a co-op placement during lunch and wouldn't be at school to check the list. P.S. This was before cell phones, text messages, and emails. A co-op placement, short for cooperative education placement, is a program where students gain practical work experience related to their field of study while still in school. It allows students to apply classroom learning in real-world settings, helping them develop skills and knowledge that will benefit them in their future careers. Gord offered to contact the school where I was working and leave a message with the secretary (they weren't called administrative assistants back then) about my status.

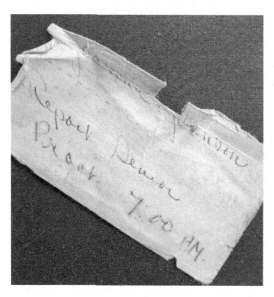

I must have checked for that message at least 300 times during the three hours I was there. A worn path had formed down the hall from the gym to the office, marked with my footsteps. Then, at 3:15 pm on that fateful day, a school secretary handed me a post-it note that changed everything. P.S. I still keep it in my wallet to this day!

At that moment, everything changed. I can't pinpoint exactly why, how, or when I truly understood it, but it did. Over the next three years, I was evolving. Not just as a better volleyball player, but I was. Not just as a leader, but I also grew into that role. Not just as a confident individual, but I filled that space too. Those three years taught me, without a doubt, that heart mattered most.   All my achievements, the player I evolved into, the captain I embodied, didn't stem from skills or bravado; it all began with heart.

First, I learned how to serve. I don't just mean serve; I mean hone the best and hardest float serve that was possible. This I could quickly control, this skill I could build and add to the team whenever they needed it. That first year, I spent the most time on the bench, watching, learning, and stepping in to serve whenever the need arose.

You would think it would have made me bitter. It didn't. I wanted to be on the court, but I knew I wasn't good enough yet, and I also knew I would be. Second, I learned how to pass. Perfectly. I watched, I learned, I practiced. Not only could I pass any serve in my vicinity, but I managed to dive my way onto the starting six the following year as I picked up *every* ball hit, tipped, or launched in my general direction. In fact, I still have a permanent callus at the base of my right palm - a comforting rough patch that will forever remind me of what made me all those years ago. Thirdly, I acquired the skill of leadership. I realized that being a captain wasn't necessary to develop this ability; what truly mattered was having confidence in my skills, trusting my teammates, and recognizing our shared, special strengths. It was during that year when my team made an incredible comeback, from a 13-5 deficit (back in the days when there were no rally points and games went to 15), to win the semi-finals against a team that, on paper, seemed superior to us. They were taller, possessed more individual talent, and were even physically stronger... but what they lacked was our collective heart. While we may have seemed unimpressive on paper, on the court, our team was pure magic. Gord Williamson, you recognized the heart we poured into our game and granted me the opportunity to make a significant impact. I am truly grateful for your support and belief in me. Thank you.

# THAT'S NOT WHAT THIS BOOK IS ABOUT. IT'S REALLY ABOUT THIS:

Can you teach heart? No. Can you help a student discover theirs? Absolutely. There are two primary motivators for learning: one is the tangible rewards - such as gaining admission to a prestigious school, receiving an award, securing a scholarship, landing a desirable job, and, let's face it, attaining the highest salary. Secondly, there's the passion for the process - realizing that continuous learning and expanding one's knowledge enriches you as an individual, a professional, a partner, and a citizen. Cultivating the "love of the game" (as depicted in the Kevin Costner movie of the same name) can be a challenging task for educators, especially in a world where everything seems like, and often truly is, a competition. P.S. I am currently writing this section while sitting across from my mom as she attempts to stop a nosebleed. We are now into the second hour. I suggested the tampon solution to her, but she's not quite ready for my brand of genius.

What's happened is that we have built entire systems centred on the concept of "winning," under the guise of "objectivity" in determining these "winners." What defines winning? Is it the highest GPA, the top MCAT score, the leading LSAT performance, or the highest SAT result? We assign importance to these scores and use them to rate our students, as if they truly reflect their intellectual abilities or their potential to achieve remarkable feats. Do I grasp the fundamental concept that in a world as immense and populated as ours, there is a need for a system that can efficiently distinguish between individuals, providing a level of organization and ranking? Of course. Here's my question.

Is the system, established during the era of the Dewey Decimal System's dominance, when knowledge was restricted by publishing agreements, and the truth was often defined by what your Grade 5 teacher proclaimed, still the same system that safeguards us in today's world?

A new generation adept at coding, accessing personal accounts of war captured from an individual's viewpoint on the other side of the world, carrying a powerful computer in the palm of their hand 24/7, and understanding that truth evolves with new information as our world advances - is this generation best suited for standardized testing?

Why is it that the visionaries and geniuses of our society have historically not been catered to by the conventional institutions designed for the general populace? How can I instill the "love of the game" in students when the game itself is evidently flawed? I initiate change by modifying elements within the existing system, shifting the classroom dynamic to engage with the journey rather than the destination.

I strive to transform the learning experience, offering students the chance to cultivate their learning process instead of solely focusing on the end result. To demonstrate my "love of the game" strategy, I will explore the three A's - Autism, Anxiety, and AI - oh my!

# AUTISM

I am not purporting to be an authority on the history, classification, or diagnosis of autism. That is not the focus of this section. What I can attest to is the increasing prevalence of education and awareness surrounding autism over the past decade, leading to noticeable shifts in classroom dynamics. Additionally, speaking as a well-informed observer, it's worth noting that the research and understanding we have today could have been instrumental in supporting children from a generation ago who were often overlooked and wrongly deemed as not smart, capable, or focused enough to excel. I often ponder how many students were demoralized by societal ignorance before they had the opportunity to make a positive impact on the world. Over the past decade, I have had the privilege of teaching numerous students, whether officially diagnosed or not, who fall on the spectrum -

including those with ADHD, ODD, diverse learning abilities, and impulse control challenges. One common thread among them all is that they are navigating a system not designed for their success. These students are essentially being compelled to bat right-handed when what they truly need is the flexibility to switch-hit. We often treat the game as an inherent structure, rarely questioning the validity of its rules. Let me provide an example of how I've attempted to reshape the game to help these students discover pathways to success... and to be fair, this approach benefits ALL students, albeit in diverse ways for each individual.

## COURSE PACKAGE ON DAY ONE:

Every student will receive a comprehensive overview of the course, outlining all major assignments and independent projects, complete with grading criteria and set deadlines for each throughout the semester. This empowers students to effectively plan and manage their academic responsibilities based on their individual lifestyles and learning capabilities. The emphasis on time management becomes a crucial aspect of their learning, demonstrating the importance of when and how each task can be completed, particularly in relation to their other academic commitments. This structured approach also provides students with the opportunity to seek additional support or insights on assignments that may pose challenges.

## EXTRA TIME ON TESTS / EXAMS:

Why do we set strict time limits on tests and exams, almost as if there's a race we're unaware of? When was the last time someone timed you with a stopwatch, demanding rapid memorization and lightning-fast writing of information? While I don't particularly favour tests and exams as primary evaluation methods, given their prevalent use in university assessments, it is my responsibility to equip students for these formats. I am not suggesting the complete removal of all time constraints; however, recognizing that high school is a critical period of brain development, it seems reasonable to provide a more flexible assessment model in this aspect. It's crucial to guide our students towards grasping what constitutes a "quality" answer, steering them away from minimalistic responses or the tendency to rewrite entire chapters under a single heading. While learning test-taking skills holds merit, expecting students to perform under high-anxiety conditions is an unrealistic and impractical expectation.

# WALKABOUTS:

Several students may struggle with excess energy or difficulty maintaining focus for extended periods (spending 70 minutes with me can be quite lively, albeit entertaining, prompting the necessity for a mental break from the amusement). After all, these are teenagers - their minds and bodies are undergoing rapid growth and transformation beyond our full comprehension. It is essential to comprehend and at times redirect the varying energies students bring throughout the day. This matter presents a dual challenge: firstly, recognizing that each student is unique, and thus understanding their individual needs and timing demands a deep understanding of who they are before devising a tailored plan. Secondly, it serves as a test of trust between teacher and student. Could they end up in the cafeteria? Could they be found shooting free throws in the gym? Could they wind up disturbing their friend in physics class? Absolutely. That's what kids are going to do. As teachers, it is our responsibility to establish clear expectations and consequences for acceptable behaviour. Equally important is the need for consistent follow-through. This can be challenging, but providing structure is key, as students thrive in a predictable environment and are more likely to meet expectations once they understand where we stand. Unless, of course, they're caught up in a dating drama - then all bets are off, sorry!

# REPEAT SUBMISSIONS:

All my students have the opportunity to submit each assignment as many times as they wish, provided it is before the established due date at the start of the semester. During my own Master's program, I had a professor who offered us this same flexibility. She shared:

"When I write a book, my editor sends it back for revisions dozens of times. Why should I expect your initial submission to be perfect? I simply require it to be submitted before the due date."

This approach enables students to learn the process of writing. Merely receiving a grade and comments without engaging in the revision and rewriting process at home does not facilitate true learning. The actual learning occurs through continuous feedback and the iterative process of revising and refining their work, just like we did with this book.

# DEBATES / PRESENTATIONS:

I provide my students with diverse options to showcase their understanding and analyze their research findings. While the traditional essay format has been predominant, there are various other ways to present knowledge effectively. Recognizing that students possess different strengths and abilities, it is my role to nurture their skills in areas where they may struggle and encourage them when they excel in their preferred methods of expression.

Allowing students to discover their passion requires giving them the space to explore how they can connect with it. This principle isn't limited to students on the spectrum or those facing learning challenges; it applies to all individuals. Recognizing and embracing this concept is crucial for enhancing the educational experience for everyone.

# ANXIETY

Why are many students facing increased levels of anxiety? Is social media a contributing factor? How can we address this issue, and why is it emerging now? The answer is quite straightforward.

Today's students, including those from the past decade, have unprecedented access to information. Moreover, students are continually exposed to a barrage of global events from various sources and at all hours of the day. Information inundates them through social media, news websites, personal vlogs, YouTube channels, and even within academic curricula and research frameworks. It truly permeates every aspect of their lives. It's tempting to blame social media platforms like TikTok and Instagram for negatively impacting our youth. It's the easy route to point fingers, complain, and advocate for bans as a quick fix.

However, if we are observant, we'll realize that we've unleashed a floodgate of influences that cannot be easily contained. It's essential to recognize the daily challenges our children face and develop a curriculum that genuinely addresses these issues. How can you determine the authenticity of what you see? How do you verify the validity of information presented to you? When should you question the accuracy of that information? How can you disconnect from the digital world and take breaks? And most importantly, how do you identify and break free from online spirals and negative cycles? All of those questions should be tackled in the classroom.

In addition, parents are also grappling with similar challenges and issues at home. Open and honest dialogues are essential for us to collectively address our new reality. Merely banning phones, blocking social media, or implementing firewalls are temporary solutions that address symptoms rather than the root problem. What our students truly need is access, information, education, and support to navigate the complex world they inhabit. P.S. Regardless of attempts to block or ban content, this generation has the skills to navigate and access the information they desire through coding and technology!

My approach to addressing anxiety extends beyond mere debate. I believe that our educational system should prioritize increased community engagement. Social media isn't solely about crafting the perfect Instagram post or a captivating TikTok video (though they hold significance - *smirk*), but rather about fostering meaningful connections. This is where the essence of "heart" lies. It is through these connections that students can engage with important issues, amplify their passions, and initiate positive change in the world. If we aim to reduce students' anxiety, we must empower them to take charge of their lives and confront their fears head-on. Isn't that the true essence of education - providing the tools to shape one's own future?

# ARTIFICIAL INTELLIGENCE (AI)

I'm about to utter words that educators worldwide dread, that parents worry about, and students view as their escape route - AI. How can we possibly educate when artificial intelligence can effortlessly sift through the vast expanse of the internet and produce essays, reports, and analyses on any subject at any complexity level? Here's my response - I'm going to embrace it. As the kids say these days, "Let it cook!" I hope I used that correctly. Oh well, moving on!

# THAT'S NOT WHAT THIS BOOK IS ABOUT

What do I mean by that? Of course, I'm not suggesting that I abandon my profession and hand over everything to AI. This is a testament to progress. Just like 15 years ago when we viewed Wikipedia with skepticism as it seemed to do all the work we wanted our students to engage in, making things seemingly too easy. So, why are we now striving to make things more challenging for our students? It's like the classic tale of "I used to walk uphill, in the snow, for 14 miles BOTH ways to get to school" and yet we find ourselves upset that our kids get a ride or take the bus. Quite ridiculous, isn't it? While AI isn't flawless, we acknowledge that it's our new reality. Instead of attempting to ban, block, or censor it - our typical response to things we don't comprehend or appreciate - we have a choice. We can choose to embrace what AI offers to our students and the world: An immensely robust, powerful, and prolific research tool. Educators must adapt by revising their traditional lesson plans, creating innovative methods to ensure that students are comprehending and critically analyzing the material presented to them. Speaking of academic integrity concerns that have existed since time immemorial, where the affluent and privileged could hire a talented individual in need of money to write their final papers. How did those students face consequences? Well, some simply inherited their fathers' businesses instead.

If I were to address this, I would introduce artificial intelligence to my students and explore its capabilities together. We would investigate what it excels at and its limitations, challenging the framework and boundaries of the program. Once we understand its potential, I would adapt the way education unfolds within my classroom. Encouraging more verbal engagement, active participation in debates, and urging students to conduct in-depth analysis during classroom sessions rather than assigning it as homework. If you're seeking the essence of education, here it is. Harness the power of the internet to access a wealth of global resources, drawing closer to truth by embracing diverse perspectives. Empower your students to question and critique the information presented to them, enabling them to participate in authentic debate and foster genuine intellectual curiosity in real-time.

Let's shift our focus from the where, what, and when to the more relevant and vital question - Why? We are now in a new era of education, where we have access to crucial information and history like never before. It's time to move beyond just studying and start analyzing and uncovering the reasons behind it all. This marks the next step in the evolution of education.

# CLASS IS IN SESSION

## FEATURED VIDEO

# 7

# TIDE IS OUT & FEAR OR FREEDOM

**My first year of** teaching was challenging, but that's not the focus of this story. This tale unfolds in the oceanside town of Tamarindo, Costa Rica, during my very first March Break as a teacher. It turned out to be the best vacation I've ever experienced, yet I almost didn't make it back. March Break in Ontario, Canada, is a week-long school holiday that takes place in March. It's a period when students and teachers take a break from their usual school schedule, giving them the opportunity to unwind, travel, or take part in different activities. This time is often favoured by families for vacations or leisure pursuits.

# TIDE IS OUT & FEAR OR FREEDOM

The trip was straightforward: learn how to surf. Shelley took the lead, and if you were friends with Shelley, you knew she was always in charge. She organized our first surf trip effortlessly - finding the country to learn in, the surf camp to register with, and the flight to catch. All I had to do was send her the cash. I think that was the best start to a vacation I have ever had. I hate planning and booking anything.

Upon our arrival, it felt like the very air was different. The gentle wind brought me peace, while the soothing sound of the waves comforted me. It seemed as if this quaint surfing town had discovered the secret to life but chose to keep it to itself. Each day was the same.

1. Wake at 8 am.
2. Homemade granola and fruit bowl for breakfast.
3. Surf lesson until noon.
4. Local, homemade lunch.
5. Surf until 5 pm.
6. Dinner at a local restaurant with a top ranking chef.
7. Asleep by 10 pm.

I'd like to point out numbers 3 and 5, both prime numbers, but that's not the main focus of this story. It's truly beautiful how math, and more specifically learning, can take place anywhere.

Have you ever surfed? Experienced that moment of getting up on a wave, perfect timing, exhilarating speed, saltwater spraying in your face, feeling the freedom of that instant? What's intriguing about surfing is the simultaneous experience of two conflicting emotions - fear and freedom. Remember these words, fear and freedom. Make a note of them nearby; they will resurface later in this book... and in your life.

# FEAR

Before catching that perfect wave, you must battle the relentless waves to reach the right spot in the ocean. You attempt to dive underneath as the wave approaches to lessen the force of the ocean. At times, you may choose to go over the wave, only to be pushed back down or crash on the other side, lifting you higher than expected. If you miss the chance to catch that perfect wave due to mistimed paddling, you have to paddle back out repeatedly until you master the most challenging skill of your life - the perfect push. Fatigued, as you catch a wave, perhaps in that weariness, you catch an edge of your board, turn too sharply into the current, lose your footing - and suddenly you bail into the ocean. The wave crashes down upon you, the undercurrents swirl you like a washing machine (a common metaphor among surfers) - flipping and pulling you upside-down until you can no longer discern which way is up to the surface. Perhaps it scrapes you across the rocky break, maybe panic sets in as your breath becomes short, perhaps you start to struggle against the powerful current, even if it's a futile effort. Fear. The moment that terrifies you the most in this sport, the very moment you feel like you might lose everything, you let go. You allow the current, wave, and pull to take you where they please. You let your body tune into the ocean instead of trying to dominate it. You anticipate the crash and the chaos. And only then, will you resurface - regaining the control you had lost. In that fear, that true panic, if you embrace it fully, you will discover one of life's greatest lessons. At times, we must release control... sometimes, we allow the current to wash over us, carrying us to a point where we can rise once more.

# FREEDOM

Now, there is that moment when you catch that wave. When your arms are strong enough to match the rhythm of the ocean. When your timing is impeccable. When you spring up onto your feet, crouched and balanced in a manner that lets you sense the wave and steer your board. As you ride atop the three, four, five foot wave (I'm no expert, not ready for those ten footers, folks) - now soaring nine to ten feet high in the air, carried by a swift and forceful wave, with ocean spray kissing your face - it's the closest I've ever come to feeling like I'm flying (and no, I won't leap out of a perfectly good plane to skydive and find out what that sensation is like - I already know how that would feel - like FALLING). I have never experienced such freedom. I have never felt so empowered. I have never felt so boundless. I hopped on the broom (and if you don't get that reference, please watch Wicked and feel a tinge of shame for missing out). Fear and liberation. Ironically, that's not the focus of this tale! Apologies for the interruption - I shall proceed.

Our surf coaches emphasized that the tide recedes at 5 pm, so it's important to exit the water by 5 pm. They advised against being on your surfboard at 5 pm, as you may be swept out to sea. They never mentioned anything about 4:50 pm. There Shelley and I sat, perched on our boards, anticipating the final wave to roll in. If I had a cell phone back then, it would have captured the perfect picture (this was in 2003 - my cell phone could only text message - AND I had to press certain buttons three times to get to the right letter). We both caught the perfect wave, rode in, pulled our boards onto the sand, and collapsed in blissful exhaustion after a fulfilling day. And then I uttered something that, in hindsight, I probably shouldn't have. Glancing at my waterproof watch, showing 4:50 pm, I turned to Shelley and said, "I'm heading out for one last ride."

Shelley laid back on her board, bidding me good luck as I ventured into the most pristine ocean you could imagine. Looking back now, the seemingly tranquil waters were actually a result of the tide going OUT. The effortless journey I had in reaching a distance far enough to catch a wave should have been a clue. BUT IT WASN'T 5 PM YET!!! As I paddled out to a sufficient distance and swung a leg over the board to sit and await the next wave, I observed a peculiarity that had escaped my notice until then. Waves had been rolling in consistently before that instant, I'd estimate every few minutes or so. In this specific moment, there was nothing... the ocean felt calm, almost motionless... the absence of waves became evident. So, I did what any rational surfer from Toronto would do - I began paddling back towards shore. If a wave wasn't going to come and carry me back, I would take matters into my own hands. Or so I thought.

And now, the true tale unfolds. As I lay prone on my board and began paddling towards the shore, I noticed something strange - I wasn't making any progress in closing the distance. I paddled with increased vigour, kicking with all my might, yet I remained stationary. Doubts crept in, questioning my own sanity, so I selected a fixed point and paddled with unprecedented intensity, only to discover at the end of my exertion that I was still in the same spot, or perhaps even more alarmingly, slightly farther out. I called out for Shelley, but she didn't budge. I could only assume that she had dozed off on her board, nestled comfortably on the shore without a worry in the world. How rude!

At this point, panic began to grip me. I abandoned my board and commenced swimming towards the shore, dragging my board along with the leash secured to my ankle. The more vigorously I swam, the more fatigued I became, and it appeared that I was drifting farther out into the ocean. Flashes of geography began to flood my mind. Tamarindo is situated on the west coast of Costa Rica, for those unfamiliar with its location. If I were to be carried away by that outgoing tide, my probable destination would be Australia. Yes, you read that correctly... take a look at a map... there's nothing but vast ocean until you reach Australia. As the perspiration from what felt like an intense workout trickled down my brow (or perhaps it was just saltwater from the ocean, but I was exerting myself to the max), and a paralyzing panic began to take hold - almost pushing me to the brink of giving up entirely - I decided to sit up on my board and make one final, desperate attempt to catch Shelley's attention. While I was shouting her name (and she remained unmoved, mind you), a lone, minuscule wave rolled in and nudged me ever so gently back towards the sandy shores of Costa Rica. It's in those moments when you contemplate surrender but choose to persevere that the magic truly unfolds. P.S. I didn't yell at Shelley on that shoreline, but she at least had to buy me dinner.

# THAT'S NOT WHAT THIS BOOK IS ABOUT. IT'S REALLY ABOUT THIS:

# THAT'S NOT WHAT THIS BOOK IS ABOUT

I am no thespian, devoid of any natural flair. Just the idea of being on stage makes me break out in a sweat. Once, in a Grade 9 Arts class, we were instructed to embody a willow tree - I dropped the class that afternoon. This one time I had to leave a murder mystery dinner show because they had the audacity to include me in the show, so I spent the rest of the night in the bathroom. Back in Grade 7, I enrolled in a modelling course where they dolled me up with a full face of makeup and had me strut with a book perched on my head - needless to say, I never went back. As a teacher, standing before students day in and day out, I grew remarkably at ease with putting on a show. If you didn't master the art of performance to captivate their attention and maintain engagement, believe me, your teaching career wouldn't last long. However, throughout my time as an educator, from my early days as a novice teacher way back in 2002, I always stayed true to myself. P.S. Let's not do the math, it's impolite!

Metro Prep Academy boasts a rich legacy of staging some of the most exceptional high school plays ever seen, all under the expert guidance of director and teacher, Ryan Seeley. Ryan's productions are not for the faint of heart. Among his repertoire are titles like Frankenstein, Of Mice and Men, The Crucible, and The Laramie Project. Each time I attended one of his plays, I left feeling mesmerized, awestruck, and often slightly perplexed, as if I hadn't quite grasped all the intricacies and depths of the performances and themes. With every show, he skillfully assembled a team of actors, set designers, lighting technicians, stagehands, and backstage managers - all aged between 13 and 19 - and orchestrated a true masterpiece. Now, wouldn't it have been nice if he had thrown in a comedy or a musical every now and then? I'll be eagerly anticipating either Rent or Wicked in my future.

# TIDE IS OUT & FEAR OR FREEDOM

For the past 21 years, without fail, I have been involved in every single one of his plays. I handle the posters, tickets, sales, promotions, intermission snacks, and t-shirt designs. And like clockwork, every year he would approach me and inquire, "So, why don't you join the cast this year, Jo?" And every year, my response remained steadfast - "Absolutely not, I'm just in charge of the merchandise." Twenty-one years of his asking, twenty-one years of my declining. And then, here comes the fearful part.

In October of 2021, fresh from the pandemic-induced shutdown that halted life for months on end, Metro embarked on rehearsals for their comeback play - "Sweat" by Lynn Nottage. As the students, under the guidance of Ryan, delved into the powerful script, I busied myself creating the poster, capturing photos, and crafting the merchandise for what promised to be one of the most impactful plays I had ever encountered. In 2022, they are building the set, perfecting blocking, securing costumes, and rehearsing lines well into the evenings passed 7 pm. Then, during March Break, the unthinkable occurs - a student must withdraw from the production. Given how far along they are in the production process, I had assumed the entire play was already set in stone. And then, Ryan does what he has always done. He requests me to step into the role. Not only does he ask me, but he adds, "Only you can pick up these lines swiftly enough to ensure this production goes on - otherwise, we might have to cancel the show." Yes, he played that card. Fortunately, for both him and me, I had recently made a significant decision in my life - to start saying "yes" to opportunities that come my way, no matter the fear or potential embarrassment. And, let's face it, he touched a chord in my teacher's heart - if I declined, I would be letting down the rest of the cast and him. So I said yes. Ryan then passed me the script and suggested, "Perhaps you'd like to read it first to grasp the full scope of my character?" I accepted the script without a safety net and confidently said yes for the second time. I wasn't scared yet. But I can promise you, I was about to be.

Have you ever read "Sweat" by Lynn Nottage? I hadn't. Nor did I have any inkling about the depth and breadth of the role I had been assigned to play. "Tracey," for the record, was one of the two central characters in the play, with roughly the second-highest number of lines in the entire production. Yes, you read that correctly - THE SECOND MOST LINES IN THE ENTIRE PRODUCTION. Curious to know how I discovered the extent of my role? I was instructed to go through the script and mark all my lines to kickstart the rapid memorization process I was about to undertake. To my surprise, THE ENTIRE BOOK WAS HIGHLIGHTED IN BLUE! Blue, evidently the preferred highlighter colour. I have since sworn off highlighters. They have been forever tainted in my eyes!

At first, the fear of performing didn't even cross my mind, which was unusual given my past avoidance of such situations. As I entered rehearsals, sat in the room, recited lines, projected my voice, delved into deep emotions, and found my rhythm with the other actors, I experienced a sense of calm. It was almost as if I had found peace in the midst of it all. Quite strange, indeed. And then, he had me stand on stage and begin blocking scenes within just a couple of weeks of going through certain acts (I barely even knew what an act was at that point, by the way). The next words Ryan uttered still send shivers down my spine: "You need to be off book." What? I'm expected to do this WITHOUT the script? And now, the sweat - the real, tangible sweat that would only appear at the mere thought of acting - returned, trickling down my back and legs (why did my legs sweat?), while every last drop of moisture seemed to evaporate from my mouth, where I actually needed it the most.

Not only was all of that true, but it was at that very moment when we transitioned from mere reading to actual acting. I can't quite convey the sheer panic that would grip me during these rehearsals. While my students had their lines memorized flawlessly and the blocking down to a tee, executing it like seasoned professionals, I was just trying to stay conscious. Here's something remarkable - the more nervous, insecure, or panicked I felt, the more supportive and incredible my students were with me. It was as if, in a single moment, they transformed into my teachers. They comforted me, rehearsed lines with me, boosted my confidence when I struggled with a scene, showed me patience, and when needed, they provided that firm push that every individual requires to reach greatness. Simultaneously, I had a coworker, a director, and a best friend of 22 years who revealed his superpowers to me. He understood my fear but never babied me, recognized my lack of experience but never made me feel inadequate, acknowledged my strong speaking abilities but also guided me on how to truly embody a character, and he knew precisely when to give me that extra nudge to step into a role he always believed I could excel in.

I have never dedicated so much effort to something I wasn't sure I could successfully accomplish in my entire life. Night after night after night, I poured my heart into it. On weekends, I scoured for the perfect outfits for "Tracey" - it was the only aspect of the entire experience where I felt at ease, so I indulged. P.S. I still have and wear those costumes in my daily life. Putting them on feels like when Superman changes in a phone booth - a transformation moment.

Was I ready for opening night? Absolutely not. Was I just as scared? Terrified. And then the curtains opened. I wish I could vividly recount that night for you, detailing each act, each scene. However, much of it is a blur as I forgot to breathe the entire time. Yet, there is one moment that stands out - a scene with Phil. It was a powerful moment where just the two of us commanded the stage, delving deep into the heart of the play. I didn't deliver my lines flawlessly on opening night (especially during that scene - Phil graciously covered for me whenever I stumbled over a line throughout the entire run), but in that particular moment, I felt a profound connection with "Tracey", with the character I was striving to embody. Surprisingly, in that moment where I expected to feel like an imposter, I experienced a sense of liberation and authenticity.

And at the conclusion of the play, as the audience showered us with love and support, a resounding "whooooaaaaa" echoed through the crowd - a sound I hadn't heard in years. Perplexed, I scanned the audience for the source of this familiar cheer, only to lock eyes with my mom seated in the front row. Typically, her presence and exuberance would be anticipated at the culmination of my achievements. However, this year, I had not expected her to attend as she had been battling cancer for most of the year and had informed me that she was too weak to make it. As a tear trickled down my face, I was overwhelmed by a rush of emotions - the fear, the liberation, and the love that only that unique blend could evoke. Now, as I teach, I find myself constantly learning. When I step in front of the class as a teacher, I am also a student. The crucial lesson I gleaned from that stage is invaluable - it motivates me to always tackle things that truly terrify me and helps me recognize when it's time to challenge my students so they can confront their fears, take the leap, and experience true freedom.

# CLASS IS IN SESSION

## FEATURED VIDEO

# LOVE & THE RIGHT PEOPLE STAY

**My parents split up** when I was three. Until I was around 13, I believed it was because my mom enjoyed watching figure skating while my dad preferred Mash - to my astonishment, that wasn't the real reason. So, from the age of three until about 16, I went on a yearly vacation with my mom and grandma to Florida. It was complete with manual windows that you had to roll down, we embarked on a 22-hour drive, and transformed it into a three-day adventure. Did we make frequent bathroom stops for my mom? Definitely. Did we ensure grandma had a constant flow of coffee during the journey? Absolutely. And did I manage to blow all my vacation money at the first mall we encountered (usually Syracuse)? Without fail, every single time. Over the span of approximately 13 years of our travels, our adventures could have easily been the basis for a hilarious "Family Vacation" book series if we had penned it (but say it with me - that's not what this book is about)!

# 1985

We made a pit stop at a gas station, somewhere in South Carolina, if memory serves me right. True to her routine, my grandmother insisted on waiting in the car while mom and I went inside to pay for the gas and grab some snacks. As I reached for the beef jerky and my mom settled the bill for the gas, out of the blue, my grandmother materialized and handed my mom money to cover the cost of the gas. We turned our heads in unison and exclaimed, "You were supposed to stay in the car." Grandma, without missing a beat, replied, "Don't worry, I locked all the doors." My immediate follow-up question was, "But where are the keys?" We then spent the next hour trying to jam a wooden spoon down the cracked window to carefully unlock the very secured car.

# 1989

We made a stop at a rest area along I-95, somewhere in Delaware. Quick side note: we all adored Delaware - fantastic mall and no sales tax. The restroom at this particular stop had a straightforward locking mechanism on a turn dial - turn left to lock, turn right to unlock. Easy enough. Mom exited first, with me following closely behind. We both headed into the travel plaza to browse for any shopping opportunities (clearly a recurring theme here).

After about 15 minutes we were starting to wonder why grandma hadn't come out yet, so back in I went. "Grandma," I shouted. In a panicked tone, my grandma exclaimed, "Jo, the door won't open!" Sensing her distress, I hurried into the adjacent stall, stood on the toilet, and reassured her, "You'll be okay, just turn the dial to the right." Angrily, she replied, "Jo, do you think I haven't been trying that?! It just won't budge!! Get help!" As I fetched an attendant, Grandma miraculously managed to open the door and stormed past us in a fit of frustration.

Upon reaching the car, my mom and I inquired why Grandma got so upset. We assured her we would have freed her eventually. With all seriousness, she replied, "I thought you were going to leave without me." We both chuckled and responded, "Do you really think we'd either abandon you or forget we brought you along on this trip?" She was left speechless at the time, but we've shared a good laugh over that moment ever since.

# 1977 - 1991

Throughout our southern adventures, we would debate whether to head directly to Florida or make a pit stop in Memphis before continuing to the happiest place on earth. The comical aspect of this was that both my mom and grandma managed to persuade me that Memphis, particularly Graceland, was EN ROUTE to Florida. It wasn't. In reality, it was an eight hour detour. They conspired to create an alternate reality for me, leading to some geographical confusion for years to come. P.S. None of that was the point of this story.

# 2000 - 2003

I came out at the age of 25. What took me so long? Probably the influence of the 90s. But that's not the focus of this story. I opened up to my friends and family quite swiftly, yet I hesitated to share this part of myself with my grandma. I'm not entirely sure why, perhaps it was because of her age, her British upbringing, her no-nonsense demeanour, or simply because I wanted to preserve our relationship without any tarnish, ever. That all changed when I bought a house with my then partner, and no I didn't tell Grandma then. I waited until we moved into the house and my partner looked me right in the eye and told me she didn't want to be gay anymore. Odd sentence, sure, but it destroyed me. And as I went up to my grandma's house to heal my very open wounds, she could tell I wasn't okay... probably the tears or the intuition... who knows. I do remember when it all changed.

I was seated on the couch beside her, likely watching a "Lethal Weapon" or "Die Hard" movie when she spotted the tear in my eye and inquired once more about why I was so distressed. I gazed at her and uttered, "My girlfriend broke up with me." In response, she did what any British grandmother would do - she gently pushed me off the couch with her forearm and declared, "Did you really think I wouldn't love you anymore?"

That was the last time we ever spoke about it. But she would judge my girlfriends heavily from then on to see if they were good enough for me.

# THAT'S NOT WHAT THIS BOOK IS ABOUT. IT'S REALLY ABOUT THIS:

# THAT'S NOT WHAT THIS BOOK IS ABOUT

In my teaching philosophy, I have always emphasized the importance of involving students' families - whether it's their parents, grandparents, cousins, guardians, or siblings. They serve as a window into each student's world, offering a connection to their identity and roots. I have always believed that to teach a student well you understand who they are. To understand them quickly, put them in a room with their family for about 15 minutes - you will get a sketch of where they have come from and who they are today, and maybe a small glimpse into who they wish to become. Because for better or worse, we are all reflections of the people who raised us, and that is the "team" you need to understand and be on from day one and that requires constant and honest communication from all parties.

Watching the dynamics play out in a family is incredibly important when understanding how to motivate, how to inspire and even how to ensure accountability to the student you teach. Some students need quiet motivation, calm and cool instruction when they feel under pressure during an exam or test. Some students need to walk for a minute, the physicality of their personality demands it. Some students need a firm command and clear deadlines to complete a task at hand. And all of that, I can read in the first family interview I sit in. So, if we are a team, this is how I structure the plays:

1. Give parents access to the material of the course - either a hardcopy OR access to the online outline that the students have access to.
2. Full assignment descriptions and their associated due dates.
3. All unit test due dates.
4. Expectations of the course and the class with clear consequence if they fail to meet them.

Why do I take on that role? Why don't I just let the student communicate the information themselves? The answer is simple - they may not be ready to do so. It's my responsibility to prepare them for that moment. Once the parents are informed of important dates, conflicts like dentist appointments, travel arrangements, and family commitments won't clash with their academic responsibilities. You wouldn't believe how many orthodontist appointments are scheduled on the same day as a unit test - it's truly frustrating.

I also need to maintain an open line of communication because children often lack control over their lives - they don't plan trips, decide when family visits for the weekend, or have a say in scheduling dentist appointments. As educators, we may jump to the conclusion that late submissions stem from the student's poor time management or lack of responsibility. However, at times, it's the external pressures and family obligations that shape their daily lives. Therefore, I strive to create an environment where all students feel supported and understood.

The team must be strong, with ongoing communication and an unbreakable bond. Without this unity, children may manipulate us against each other indefinitely - not because they are wicked or evil, but because it's part of their nature. Have you ever heard the story of the scorpion and the frog? In the tale, the scorpion asks the frog for help crossing the river. The frog hesitates, knowing the scorpion's nature to sting. The scorpion reassures him, explaining that if he stung the frog, they would both drown. Despite this, the scorpion ends up stinging the frog. Why? Because it's in his nature. I'm not likening students to scorpions or anything of the sort, but when faced with a choice between attending history class or going to lunch at McDonald's with the person they have a crush on, history class will inevitably lose every single time. That's perfectly fine though. I don't hold it against them for indulging in stolen lunches and skipping classes - it's all part of being a kid, creating memories along the way. However, my role is to mitigate the negative consequences of those skipped lunches and ensure they make it to history class more often than not. And sometimes, they're just hanging out in the gym.

Now, here's the true reason why parents and teachers must come together as a team - it's crucial when significant mistakes are made, when a child faces trauma and pain, when they feel lost and have nowhere to turn - that's when an exceptional team is essential. Whether it's dealing with skipped tests, plagiarized assignments, classroom breakdowns, heartbreak from crushes, or the continuous assault on their self-esteem and confidence, having a strong team is vital. So, as soon as we come up against a problem - as soon as that student is facing an issue - I make the call, I assemble the team. It's kind of like "The Avengers" but we don't get lycra outfits or a jet. I also ensure that the student understands that when I make that call, it's a part of our ongoing conversation and discussion. I make sure they recognize that they are an integral part of the team, so it doesn't come across as adults trying to control their lives, but rather as a way to support their growth and development. There are days when students have done horribly stupid things, things they regret, things they wish they could take back and I tell those students I am going to make the call. They will face the consequences of the stupid thing they did and they will get through it and we will move on - as a team. There are other days, very very few days, where the student doesn't get it, is still angry, is still unaware of the thing they did, isn't ready to accept it, in fact fights it and argues about it and denies it, and I tell them I'm going to make the call. They will face the consequences of the thing they did, they will have to come to terms with it, they will have to accept it and they will get through it and we will move on - as a team. My grandma was a huge part of my team. And even though she is no longer with us, as I type this with tears in my eyes, she remains an irreplaceable part of my team and will always hold that special place in my heart. Memories of elephants, casinos, "Die Hard" movies, car rides, and affectionate gestures will forever remind me of our bond and the love we shared.

## CLASS IS IN SESSION

### FEATURED VIDEO

# DRESS CODE & EMPOWER, DON'T PROTECT

After nearly a decade in my teaching career, just when I believed I had everything under control, a 15-year-old humbled me and imparted a crucial lesson. I occasionally struggle with active listening... truth be told, it's still a work in progress. I find myself caught up in the desire to win arguments, to prove my point, and to rely on my quick wit to outshine my opponent. At 35, I wasn't smart enough to shut up… but we all have our revelatory moments.

# DRESS CODE & EMPOWER, DON'T PROTECT

Back in 2010, the halls of Metro Prep were painted in a different colour, the artwork displayed highlighted different pieces, and the building itself had a different vibe compared to today - even the culture was different. The school had implemented a dress code for our students, a measure that most people would have understood. Students had been accustomed to having their hats taken off their heads for the past few years, so it didn't really faze most of them. The issue with this dress code was its primary focus on the female students, as is often the case with many dress codes. Cut-off shirts, short shorts, and "Flashdance" attire were very popular at the time (feel free to look it up if you're not familiar with the reference). It then became our responsibility to enforce these rules. Honestly, I believed I was doing a noble deed by safeguarding our female students from the male gaze or the potential dangers of the world around them. I understand that my perspective may not come across positively here... just give me a moment to explain further.

One day, one of my young female students asked if she could speak to me after class. This conversation, filled with honest truths, truly opened my eyes. Here's how it unfolded: "Jo, can we talk about the dress code?" Stephanie quietly asked. I replied, "Of course, Steph, whatever you need." "Why do we have a dress code? What is its purpose?" She asked softly once more. I responded with what I believed was a common-sense answer, "Well, young girls need to be mindful of what they wear in this world. It's filled with risks and dangers. Relying on your attire to boost self-esteem or attract attention can be problematic and may result in serious consequences." I know, I know. I understand your concerns, please continue reading.

Steph leaned back in her chair, pondered my response, took a deep breath, and then shared her thoughts, "But everyone's self-esteem is tied to what they wear. Kids throughout this school are exploring their identities and how they wish to express themselves - some genuinely, while others are just experimenting. But to point out that young girls don't have that option, that they aren't intelligent enough, self aware enough or brave enough to decide that for themselves you limit them. You decide for them who they are. You take away their agency to have the discussion or decide for themselves. You make them weaker." I sat up, began to speak, but she interrupted me with this:

"Also, why are we responsible for what men might think or what criminal acts they might do to us based on what we wear? Why should someone else's failings as a responsible person dictate who we are or how we present ourselves? What if my opinion elicits a violent response? I know you wouldn't stand for that. But the size of the straps of my tank top are cause for personal liability? My job isn't to make myself smaller, more invisible or more palatable for anyone - my job should be figuring out who I am and how I wish to stand in this world."

My mouth dropped, my eyes widened, and the words that usually came so easily suddenly escaped me. I don't recall ever being rendered speechless before this conversation or since. I leaned back in my chair, still silent, grappling to find a response to the incredibly brave, intelligent, and articulate student before me. My words of wisdom, once I could muster an actual voice, were quite simple. "You are absolutely right."

I believe she was prepared for a debate, so when those words were spoken, she seemed taken aback, glancing around the room in confusion before meeting my eyes again as I chose to elaborate further. After giving that one sentence a moment to resonate, I proceeded with this: "I believe I was raised in a generation that misguided me. I've viewed myself as your protector rather than someone who should empower you. I've felt it was my duty to shield you from all challenges rather than assist you in becoming resilient enough to confront them on your own. I wanted to stand in front of you rather than beside you. And I now realize that was a mistake. From this day forward, I am committed to doing better."

# THAT'S NOT WHAT THIS BOOK IS ABOUT. IT'S REALLY ABOUT THIS:

One might assume I wouldn't have needed to learn this lesson. One might assume I should have been intelligent, perceptive, and informed enough to see beyond the clothing to the person, to recognize how significant our attire is to the individual we are. One might assume. Oh, come on now! I sport a sideways hat (with more hats in my collection than you could fathom), baggy jeans, vibrant graphic tees, I handpick my shoes from a wall I painted and designed myself, an array of jackets that I've lost count of, and a massive collection of oversized watches (yes, I may be compensating a bit). What I wear and how I wear it is a reflection of who I am, and it has sparked debate every time I post a video or enter a room. Let's be real, my fade triggers hostility on a daily basis. I acknowledge that my style and self-presentation challenge their core concepts of masculinity and femininity - the gender norms we readily link to them. I also grasp that this fundamentally disrupts the most basic social constructs they have been ingrained with - it always comes down to the hair.

Reflecting on it, despite defying societal expectations, I sense that I was also conforming to them simultaneously. It has long been deemed acceptable for girls to embrace tomboyish traits, don hats, play baseball, aspire to be doctors - roles historically reserved for men -

because, as per societal norms, we are progressing, evolving, with masculinity seen as the pinnacle. Isn't that peculiar? Here lies the crux of sexism - the real discrimination isn't about the division of labour, traits, or even clothing; it's about the preference of one over the other - it's the notion that the masculine is superior. Rational over emotional. Doctor over nurse. Pants over skirts. So, when I dress the way I do, at least to a certain extent (though the hair seems to be a sticking point for many), I am elevating myself, I am progressing, I am conforming to the model of success. Here lies the major problem... we link gender to sex and then establish a hierarchy. Gawd, aren't we foolish? And apparently, just because I shattered one mold doesn't mean I shattered them all. The remnants of patriarchy in my upbringing ingrained in me the notion to shield women who may not be able to shield themselves. It critiqued their attire, the makeup they wore, and the height of their heels. It instilled in me to prioritize the rational over the emotional, to be fuelled by competition while undervaluing cooperation. As a teacher, I've had to confront that bias, particularly while sporting my sideways hat and baggy pants.

In September of 2017, Kansas University hosted the "What Were You Wearing?" student survivor art installation in the student union. The exhibit featured 18 outfit displays, each paired with survivors' narratives. The aim of the exhibit was to challenge the prevalent rape myth that suggests a woman's attire places her at risk, thereby shifting the responsibility for her safety onto her rather than the perpetrator of the assault. As a teacher on a journey of learning and one who recognizes the transformative power of art in shaping the world, this exhibit arrived at a crucial moment for both. It paved the way for classroom dialogues and self-reflection among all my students. I candidly addressed my biases and how my inclination towards protection sometimes hindered the path to empowerment. My own socialization had obstructed what was fair and equitable. It's truly remarkable what can be achieved when you acknowledge your biases, your subjectivity, your shortcomings as an adult, and openly navigate through them with the next generation.

As for a dress code at school, let me be clear. Of course there are clothes that fit different occasions - I've had to learn how to transform my style into one that fits a Vice Principal, baggy jeans and a backwards hat just doesn't make the cut anymore. Does that mean I sacrifice my identity and blindly conform to societal norms? Not at all. It means exploring new styles that blend my authentic self with a more formal, business-appropriate look. While my students are subject to dress expectations, my stance is that these standards should be fair and consistent for all. For instance, a rule like "no beer shirts" should apply universally - regardless of who you are, it's best not to wear clothing that came from a case of beer in public. Is it easy? Of course not, students love to push that envelope, so I have devised a new plan.

I have recently started creating Metro Prep School Gear. Think of it as a school uniform that meets the runway, streetwear meets the physics classroom, community meets individuality. I don't want to eradicate the individual, but I am interested in creating a team. And my team is going to look outstanding. P.S. By the time this book comes out you will be able to buy all Metro Gear on our website - you can be on our team if you want.

www.metroprep.com

# CLASS IS IN SESSION

## FEATURED VIDEO

# POSTFACE

# METRO'S CLOSING

**My school, Metro Prep** Academy in Toronto, is a prestigious private high school known for its rigorous academic programs and supportive learning environment. The school focuses on providing personalized education to help students excel academically and develop critical thinking skills. With a strong emphasis on individualized attention and small class sizes, Metro Prep Academy aims to nurture students' intellectual curiosity and prepare them for success in higher education and beyond. The school also offers a variety of extracurricular activities and opportunities for students to explore their interests and talents outside the classroom. I have dedicated my entire adult life to teaching at Metro Prep Academy, the only school where I have ever taught. During my practice teaching year, my associate teacher had a habit of mysteriously disappearing whenever I assumed control of the class, citing personal tasks such as mowing the lawn, walking the dog, or simply taking a nap. This puzzling scenario remains a true story that never fails to intrigue me. What a time to be alive! Many have questioned why I chose to work at a private school, especially considering my strong advocacy for unions and a fully funded public educational system. The secret answer to this question? I will reveal it exclusively here: Metro gave me a job.

At the dawn of the century, securing a teaching job was not easy and the public board wasn't hiring at the time. Eventually a friend of a friend said they could get my resume in front of the right eyes to hopefully get me an interview.     But it was in the interview, or thereafter, I knew I was supposed to work at Metro.   P.S. That's not what this story is about, but I think you need to hear the story anyway. I walked into Metro with absolutely no knowledge of what kind of school I was entering. Nevertheless, with a full heart, I proceeded. Wayne, the owner and principal, greeted me, and my task that fateful day was a simple job interview. As I sat down, we discussed the school, my reasons for teaching, strengths, weaknesses... all the usual and expected topics that every interview covers. Little did I know, this interview was about to take an unexpected turn.

I took a seat in front of a kindly older gentleman, who had a heavyset build and gentle eyes. His eyes remained hidden behind his glasses until after a few minutes when he finally lifted them to introduce himself. The interview began in a room brimming with books, from floor to ceiling, a massive desk cluttered with papers and file folders, and the soft bubbling of a fish tank behind me creating a soothing background ambiance. The first 20 minutes of the interview unfolded predictably, with routine questions, standard responses, and smiles exchanged on cue. However, everything changed in an unexpected way... a turn I had no inkling was coming, catching me completely off guard. As Wayne glanced down at my resume, he posed a question that shifted the tone of the conversation: "What was the focus of your Master's Thesis?" I confidently replied, "The revitalization of teachers' unions in the new international economic and educational climate." However, it soon became clear that my answer was not what he had expected... and then, something unexpected happened.

Wayne, who had experience in a unionized setting, began to express his views on the perceived negative impact of teacher's unions, citing concerns about a culture of complacency and prioritizing personal needs over student welfare. In response, I passionately defended the achievements of unions, highlighting their role in shaping labour laws, advocating for human rights, and ensuring fair treatment for teachers in terms of pay and protection against discrimination by employers. We fought for a full 40 minutes. Voices raised, veins popping out of my forehead, aggressive arm gestures - it was intense. After the heated exchange, I left feeling dazed and confused. How did things escalate so quickly? Why didn't anyone warn me about the intensity of the situation? And what was I going to do about securing a job now? As I sat in my car, grappling with the aftermath of blowing my first major job interview, I did what any person would do - I called my mom.

I reflected on the intense exchange during the interview, feeling the weight of the confrontation and doubting my chances of securing the job. Overwhelmed, I held back tears and whispered to myself, "There is no way I am getting that job." Interestingly, that phone call in 2002 ended up costing me around $34, back when phone plans weren't as common. And then, two weeks later, the unexpected happened. Wayne's voice came through on the other end of the line, offering me the job. Shocked and bewildered, I swiftly accepted his offer, hung up the phone, and sat in quiet disbelief. It's funny how that interview ended up shaping one of the most important lessons I learned as both a teacher and a student. I realized that the best education thrives in environments where debates can unfold freely and openly, without the constraints of politeness but with a strong foundation of respect. Every idea is open to debate, and all well-informed perspectives are not only valid but also encouraged. Education often leads us down a challenging and imperfect path, yet it remains the most valuable journey to embark upon. This foundation will prove essential for what lies ahead.

# THAT'S NOT WHAT THIS BOOK IS ABOUT. IT'S REALLY ABOUT THIS:

The year 2024 brought about unexpected changes. I wasn't ready. I should have been prepared. I should have had a backup plan. I should have explored all my options, but I didn't. I believe Ryan was the only one who truly saw me as a leader at school. I was a respected teacher who took my Grade 7 and 8s on exciting adventures, developed a unique curriculum for them, performed my job diligently, coached volleyball with decency, led students on educational trips worldwide to foster learning and community building, and remained loyal to my community. However, I'm not sure if anyone, myself included, ever viewed me as a leader in that school. It's intriguing how we can begin to perceive ourselves based on how we believe others see us. Do you see the issue here? I'm not entirely certain I recognized it, at least not clearly. I believe I allowed this perception to shape me more than I would have preferred, if I'm completely honest. I failed to notice the problem, the boundaries, the constraints that I unwittingly allowed to confine me.

I remained oblivious to it all until life compelled me to confront it. It's funny how life has a way of bringing things into focus, isn't it? Wayne was a man whose identity was intertwined with his school, his unwavering commitment to students, education, his school, and his staff. Despite his health declining over six years prior, Wayne brushed off the need for rehabilitation. Even when we had to relocate the entire school just before the pandemic and he fell ill again, he shrugged it off. As his mobility became a challenge and his energy waned, he continued to ignore it. The only thing that held significance for him was being seated behind his desk and overseeing the operations of the school. He even disregarded the small cancerous spots on his skin, refusing to go to the hospital for additional medications or treatments. He turned a blind eye to all of it until he was finally admitted to the hospital in February 2024.

I sensed the severity of the situation when he was absent from school for over a week, and it became even more apparent when he invited me to visit him in the hospital. He never let me before, not once. When I went into his room he seemed more Wayne then I've seen him in a long time. Wayne, despite his health struggles, maintained his sense of humour by laughing and joking about the tattoos on my arm, which he often teased me to wash off. We engaged in lively debates about politics and world events, and he even requested a Diet Coke. To my surprise, I discovered that Wayne, the same boss who scoffed at my tattoos, actually had one on the back of his shoulder. When I pointed out his tattoo, he simply chuckled, perhaps blushing a bit, and remarked, "The debate was good for you." As I prepared to leave, assuming he was on the road to recovery, he asked me, "Are you heading straight home tonight?" I chuckled and replied, "Of course, Wayne. It's already 8:30 pm on a Thursday, I have to teach tomorrow, and I'm usually in bed by 9 pm." He gently touched my arm and suggested, "Don't head straight home, go out for dinner and then hit the dance floor. Or skip dinner altogether and just go dancing." I paused at his unexpected comment, smiled, and assured him that I would visit him soon and urged him to recover quickly as his desk was missing him. As I exited the hospital room, I couldn't shake off the peculiar feeling his words left me with, but I carried on home, hoping for the best. Within a few days of our meeting, he passed away. Just like that.

We didn't even have a chance to pause, to grieve, or to feel his absence before we were thrust into a whirlwind of change. Just a few weeks after his passing, we were informed that Metro would be closing down. His family wasn't equipped or willing to take on everything the school would have required to stay afloat.

# MAY 1, 2024

That's when Ryan turned to me and asked a straightforward question, "Are you finished?" "Nope. Are you?" I replied. "Nope," he answered. And in that moment, without much hesitation or concern for the logistics, we embarked on a mission to find a way to save Metro. I suppose we always understood the *why*… so we took a leap of faith, trusting that the safety net would materialize beneath us.

Right after that meeting, we reached out to every possible person we thought might be interested in starting or rescuing a school. We spent our days in back-to-back meetings, endless phone calls, and countless discussions. While I taught history and passionately discussed saving the school, Ryan was busy directing a play (a remarkable production of Frankenstein, to be exact) and advocating for the school's preservation.

Ryan and I successfully crafted a plan that involved a new owner and a new building, while preserving the ethos of Metro that both the staff and families relied on. To unveil our plan and gauge interest, we organized a town hall meeting. To accommodate all parents, we scheduled two nights for the meeting - on Tuesday and Thursday of the same week.

# Town Hall Meeting Part 1: May 7, 2024

In a packed meeting in the school cafeteria, we spoke to both current and prospective parents (for the upcoming semester) about the school closure, which had been announced via email on May 3rd. Ryan and I then took the floor to outline our proposed plan to relocate Metro to a new site with fresh partners, all while maintaining the core values and ethos of Metro Prep. The plan was new and the building was under renovation, so in essence we were asking these parents to just trust us. The most heartwarming moment of the meeting was when parents expressed their unwavering support by saying they would "follow us anywhere" and even offered to set up tents for us to continue teaching. It was a truly touching moment when, almost as if by magic (or perhaps not so sudden after all), I saw a united front before us - a dedicated team of individuals ready to follow us wherever we chose to lead.

What lay ahead was going to be more than just okay - it was going to be truly epic. Standing beside Ryan, I could sense the magnitude of what was to come. Though I couldn't quite visualize it clearly because everything seemed so chaotic and hazy, I could feel the promise of an extraordinary future. I also experienced a sense of what it truly meant to step into a leadership role, to walk in the shoes of a leader, or perhaps don the hat of a leader - the metaphor may be a bit fuzzy, but you catch my drift. It was like catching a wave - I didn't control the ocean, but I somehow managed to ride it at just the right moment, tapping into my instincts. Was I scared? Absolutely. But amidst the fear, I also felt a profound sense of liberation and freedom.

## Town Hall Meeting Part 2: May 9, 2024

By the time of the second meeting, there had been a significant shift. We were now looking at the potential involvement of a new investor, who happened to be the owner of the building we currently occupied. The night before, Ryan and I had a lengthy two-hour discussion about this very prospect. As we unveiled this development to the packed cafeteria of parents, we were met with an even greater outpouring of support and encouragement. However, it was important to note that nothing was set in stone - our location, our partnerships, and our future still remained somewhat uncertain and hazy at best.

## Post Meetings Pre-Frankenstein

Over the following weeks, Ryan and I found ourselves in a state of uncertainty. We were unsure if we were leaving, staying, if the school was up for sale, or if it wasn't. It felt like a whirlwind of confusion, but amidst it all, I didn't feel afraid. The future was a blank canvas - would we relocate? Would we remain? How would we manage to accomplish everything by September? These questions loomed large, but the path ahead remained unclear. As we pondered the uncertainties, one pressing question lingered: how many students would we lose in the process? Then, in the waning days of May, we received not just one, but a series of calls from our potential partner in Vancouver - a visionary CEO from an esteemed genetics company. This individual expressed a keen interest in collaborating with Ryan and I to establish a school that would be truly unique. The goal was to build upon our existing ethos and craft an educational institution unlike any other, setting a new standard in the field. P.S. Amidst all the unfolding events, Ryan and I were also busy organizing a trip to Ireland for 14 students.

P.P.S. Reflecting on the transformative experiences of traveling the world with students and the profound lessons learned along the way, I can't help but think there's potential for a second book capturing these adventures and the impact they had on both the world and ourselves.

# Opening Night - Frankenstein: May 30

And so, on May 30, 2024, during the opening night of Frankenstein, Ryan and I had the joyous opportunity to reveal some exciting news. While we hadn't acquired Metro Prep, we successfully preserved our namesake, secured our place in the building, and forged a partnership with an individual who possessed a deep passion for education, STEM (with a new genetics lab on the horizon), and the arts in a way that truly amazed us. The cheers reverberating through the hall were truly epic, resonating deep within my soul. In a whirlwind of events, I witnessed the performance of Frankenstein, embarked on a journey to Ireland, and then found myself in a partnership to lead an entire school. As the saying goes, the past serves as a prologue to the remarkable chapters yet to unfold.

# 2025 and Beyond

As we navigate through life, it's essential to frame our experiences in a way that propels us towards a better and brighter future. Each moment, whether joyful or challenging, offers valuable lessons and opportunities for growth. By reflecting on our past experiences with a positive outlook, even during the dark times, we can extract wisdom, resilience, and insight that will guide us towards a more fulfilling tomorrow. Embracing the power of framing our experiences optimistically allows us to shape a narrative that inspires hope, fuels ambition, and paves the way for a future filled with possibilities and success. As a dedicated educator and passionate administrator at Metro Prep Academy, I take immense pride in the work that we do and the impact we have on shaping the minds and futures of our students. Every day, I am committed to fostering a nurturing and inspiring learning environment where students can thrive academically, socially, and emotionally. My role at Metro Prep Academy is not just a job; it is a calling that I wholeheartedly embrace with enthusiasm and dedication. I am honoured to be a part of this vibrant educational community, and I look forward to continuing to make a positive difference in the lives of our students and the school as a whole.

Never could I have fathomed that a global pandemic would bring the world to a standstill. However, amid the chaos and uncertainty, I found solace in the guidance and wisdom of those who have shaped my experiences. From the iconic 70's orange snowsuit to Mrs. Lichacz's infectious belly laugh at my mom's hospital, and from Ray's Hall and Oates dance moves to his impressive comic collection and scare pranks, each memory has contributed to equipping me with the resilience and adaptability needed to navigate through unprecedented challenges. Surprisingly, what started as a few lighthearted dance videos shared on TikTok has blossomed into an online community of millions of individuals who meet regularly to learn, live and laugh together. This unexpected turn of events not only brought joy and connection during difficult times but also highlighted the power of positivity and creativity in fostering a sense of unity and support across virtual platforms. The journey from unforeseen circumstances to unexpected opportunities has reinforced my belief in the importance of embracing change, finding strength in community, and staying open to the endless possibilities that life may present.

## THAT'S NOT WHAT THIS BOOK IS ABOUT

While my sphere of influence has expanded from a few hundred students to encompass large conference audiences, book studies, workshop groups, school teams, and now millions of people online, one fundamental truth remains unchanged: the profound impact of genuine connection and authentic storytelling. Whether engaging with a classroom of eager learners or a global community of diverse individuals live on YouTube, the power of human connection and the art of storytelling continue to bridge gaps, inspire change, and foster a sense of unity across all boundaries. As my reach extends further and my platform grows larger, I hold steadfast to the belief that at the core of every interaction lies the potential to inspire, uplift, and make a meaningful difference in the lives of others.

# THAT'S WHAT THIS BOOK IS ABOUT.

# CLASS IS IN SESSION

## FEATURED VIDEO

# ABOUT THE AUTHOR

## JOANNA JOHNSON

Student, Teacher, School Leader, TikTok'er, Podcaster, Shoe and Hat Collector, Buffy Fanatic, Political Activist and Human Rights' Advocate. Biographies only show who we were – let's have a conversation so we can figure out who we are.

## www.unlearn16.com
## @unlearn16

# CONSULTING & KEYNOTE SPEAKING

To learn more about Joanna Johnson or to book her for a visit to your school, district, conference or event, visit:

## www.unlearn16.com

**Inspire ● Innovate ● Lead ● Teach ● Learn**

# CODE BREAKER INC.

**Our mission is simple.** Engaging students. Well, it is even more than that. We believe in investing in students' well being. We believe in educating the entire child - mind, body, and soul. We are working to change parameters to meet the needs of ALL students. We believe that all students can achieve if given a fair chance. We accomplish our goals by creating content. We blog, we tweet, we YouTube, we attend conferences, we lead workshops, we develop professional development programs to meet the needs of full school districts. We are passionate about inspiring educators to create curious seeking individuals in classrooms built on a community of trust, risk-taking and a freedom to fail.

Breaking code isn't just about programming or AI, it's about disrupting the status quo. It is about challenging social norms. It is about having critical conversations. It is about challenging systematic beliefs. It is about educating the whole child - mind, body, and soul. Code Breaker Inc. is a beautifully dangerous invitation to reflect on education.

Browse our selection of BEST SELLING books or submit your own manuscript at:

## www.codebreakeredu.com

www.unlearn16.com

www.codebreakeredu.com

Made in the USA
Las Vegas, NV
30 June 2025

24249546R00085